Further praise for *Up*

'This crisp book recaptures common sense in a way that is both very practical and intensely personal. On every page, you'll find yourself saying 'I really must do that.' Buy it now!'
Stephen Robertson, Director General, British Retail Consortium

'John Timpson says it like he sees it and pulls few punches. His story, his vision, and his simple, practical ideas should make all business people stop and think.'
Luke Mayhew, former Chairman of Pets at Home and former MD of John Lewis Partnership

'A refreshing, no-nonsense business book – a must read.'
Charles Dunstone, CEO, Carphone Warehouse

ABOUT THE AUTHOR

John Timpson is the Chairman of Timpson Ltd, his family business. With 850 stores across the UK, Timpson is one of the best-established names on the British high street. The company was one of the original Sunday Times Top 10 Companies to Work for. It has also been named Retail Employer of the Year, and is in the J P Morgan Family Business Hall of Fame. John was appointed CBE in 2004 for 'services to the retail sector'.

Upside Down Management

A Common Sense Guide to Better Business

John Timpson

A John Wiley & Sons, Ltd., Publication

CONTENTS

ACKNOWLEDGEMENTS

Stuart and Matthew Rock of Real Business encouraged me to start writing a regular business column 11 years ago. As a result, writing has become a hobby that has brought me hours of enjoyment every month.

I am grateful to Ellen Hallsworth who had the courage to commission this book and to Christine Hickman who typed every draft (there have been a few).

The content of this book owes a lot to the determination of my son, James, our Managing Director, who has put many of my ideas into practice and invented many more of his own.

My biggest 'thank you' is to my wife, Alex, who has not only allowed me the time to write the book (with far fewer complaints than I expected) but has also supplied an amazing instinct and moral compass that has had a major influence on my career and our business philosophy.

Acknowledgements

*   *   *   *   *

All royalties from the book will go to After Adoption, a charity that is growing rapidly from its Manchester base, providing fantastic help to adoptive parents, adopted children and their birth parents.

PREFACE

Until the age of 29 I expected to spend all my working life in a family-run public company of shoe shops. Due to fate, and a lot of luck, I now own a national chain of shoe repairers. It has been a turbulent journey.

In 50 years the shoe repair market has declined by 90%. Of the 35,000 shoe repair shops and workshops that existed in 1960, only 3,500 remain. By diversifying into key cutting, engraving, watch repairs, photoprocessing and dry cleaning, Timpson has not only survived but has consistently strengthened. We now have over 850 branches and are growing more quickly than ever before.

Adding extra services alongside shoe repairs helped us to survive, but the real secret behind our success is the quality of the colleagues who serve our customers. That's why I believe that what I've learned at Timpson may be of some use to other business leaders, executives and entrepreneurs.

It took me 22 years as a Chief Executive to discover how to create great customer care. Since then our business has literally been turned upside down – that's why I call the Timpson style 'Upside Down Management'. Timpson colleagues enjoy a level of trust and freedom that doesn't exist in any other multiple retailer. I've been called a maverick, but I haven't done any of this just to be different. Sales and profits have grown rapidly since we had the courage to give shop colleagues the freedom to choose the way they run their branch. Turning your business upside down is good for the bottom line.

Our style of Upside Down Management has made me aware of the modern techniques and forms of 'best practice' that get in the way of good business. Management science has gone too far. Too many people are promoted simply because they obey the rules, and many managers are afraid to use their initiative.

It's time we blew the whistle on all this top-down management; we need fewer directives and less red tape. Managers should cancel meetings and visit the real world to find out what's going on. Instead of relying on consultants, they should listen to the people who actually do the job.

I've written this book in the hope that some people will have the courage to enter the world of Upside Down Management that I have inhabited for the past 12 years. It is an attempt to encourage fellow entrepreneurs to break the rules. In some respects it is a manifesto for business run by common sense.

Every business has a tale to tell, and all business lessons ought to come from real-life experience. A fair portion of this book is the Timpson story, explaining how a shoe shop opened by my great grandfather in the 1860s has developed into an 850-shop service chain with an annual turnover of over £150 million. It is nearly 50 years since I started in the business, and although I've made plenty of mistakes, I've learned a lot of lessons along the way.

I've tried to litter the book with numerous ideas that may be relevant to other businesses. I also discuss how to select people with personality and how to praise them; how to deal with poor performance and how to develop new ideas. I have been dangerously frank; age brings the benefit of being candid. I've tried to cover some of the things I would never have dreamt of mentioning 25 years ago – the bad decisions, the difficult times, coping with stress – and some of the things I regret. We can learn as much, if not more, from mistakes as we can from stories of success.

I hope there is plenty of passion in the book, particularly in our approach to ethical trading and corporate social responsibility. And, I hope I give the impression that it's been great fun. As Alex, my wife, has told me on many occasions: 'If you don't enjoy it, why bother?'

I've enjoyed being a maverick and still do, and I hope this book will encourage you to try Upside Down Management. If you do, I promise that you will not be disappointed. I also hope to see a change in attitude to authority. We need entre-preneurs with the strength of character to ignore red tape, best practice and official guidelines – business needs people with flair who have the determination to put administrators in their proper place.

This book has no rules, it's just common sense.

John Timpson
Wythenshawe, Manchester, 2010

Chapter One

THE TIMPSON EXPERIENCE

Perhaps I shouldn't have slammed the boardroom door but it seemed to be the best way to end the most traumatic time of my life.

My career path was clear cut from an early age. I was born into a family business which I joined as soon as I left school. At the age of 27 I was a director of the publicly quoted William Timpson Limited and two years later, in 1972, I felt I had become a fixture on the board. Although the business was facing a few difficulties, our September meeting was quieter than normal. I looked round the table at my fellow directors – there was no hint of controversy and less than the usual level of tension.

My father, a straightforward, honest man, was thrust into the Chair after his uncle and father had died within three months of each other without leaving a clear line of succession. Snapping at his heels was his cousin, Geoffrey Noakes, the Chief Executive. Geoffrey's military background dictated his style of management: every employee was expected to follow his standing orders.

1

The cousins were complete opposites, neither of them appreciating the other's strengths and never working as a team. My father was comfortable to be the caretaker of the family business and had a strong rapport with the staff, but no passion for ideas. Geoffrey, on the other hand, wanted change. He dreamt of being the top dog and, to further his ambition, recruited Professor Roland Smith as a non-executive director. Although based at a business school, the Professor was developing a new career outside university, offering advice to companies not just through consultancy but also as a member of their board. He collected a number of directorships and was later involved in controversy at The House of Fraser and British Aerospace. He was using his professorial platform to promote a climate of change. He certainly had a stronger character than most of the others round the table.

Bob Kirkman, a Scottish accountant who had recently been appointed Finance Director, seemed technically able, very precise and particularly polite. But I wasn't sure whether his loyalty lay with Geoffrey or my father.

The Personnel Director, Bill Simmons, was the oldest man on the board. He had started as a shop boy and rose up through area management with a tough reputation for strong discipline. He ruled the field staff with a rod of iron. His son, Alan, the men's shoe buyer, was one of three other directors appointed on the same day as I was. The move had been designed to strengthen the business, but in retrospect it made the board too big and drove us into detail rather than strategy. Norman Redfern was responsible for property – Norman was one of Geoffrey's men, working in a property department that preferred to chase new shops in north-western suburbs like Benchill, Wythenshawe and Belle Vale, Liverpool, rather than have the courage to acquire big city centre shops that the company desperately needed. The last member of the board was Bert Brownhill, another military man, who ran the computer department. In those days appointing an IT Director was seen as trendy, but Bert was not a trendy man, being best described as a 'safe pair of hands'.

Privilege still reigned supreme at Timpson. Looking back it's difficult to imagine how different the corporate world was a few decades ago. As in most companies in those days, dining was strictly segregated. Your place in the pecking order was determined by whether you ate in the general canteen, or the dining rooms allocated to either the junior and senior executives, or the directors.

After the board meeting, we sat round a coffee table in the director's dining room drinking sherry while a waitress took our order. I saw the Professor lean across to my father and whisper a quiet remark, but I didn't take much notice. Over lunch, discussion ranged from the high level of inflation to the poor start to Manchester City's season. After dessert, instead of returning to sit in the armchairs for coffee, my father, Geoffrey and the Professor disappeared, leaving me with the other directors, who quietly peeled off much earlier than usual. Bob Kirkman, the last to leave, asked whether I could come down to his office in 15 minutes. As soon as I walked through his office door I realised that this was not a casual encounter. Bob was sitting with Bill Simmons and Bert Brownhill – and got straight to the point: 'While we're meeting you, Geoffrey and Roland Smith are seeing your father to suggest that he should step down as Chairman.' They went on to explain that this was the right thing for the business and that my father would be offered the honorary title of President, but would play no further part in the company.

I didn't hear much more, I was simply stunned. My mind was racing. I hadn't really trusted my fellow directors and my lack of faith was now confirmed. I didn't stay for a discussion, I went straight upstairs to see my father, but the sign on his door said 'engaged'. I returned to the dining room, poured myself another sherry and sat in deep contemplation. Half an hour later I found my father in his office. He was with Teresa, his secretary for the past 15 years, and I had never seen him more determined. He had made it clear to Geoffrey and Roland Smith that he would not retire, and they had made it equally clear that he had two weeks to decide otherwise he would be forced to go.

When I got home that night, my wife, Alex, was even more determined than my father. Her sharp political antenna had warned her for some time that Geoffrey would steamroll the rest of the board and gain control of the business. 'You're going to be busy over the next few weeks,' said Alex. 'You had better start now.'

At Alex's suggestion I went to see Geoffrey at his home that night. After a superficially warm greeting we went to his library where he poured a drink which gave me the courage to be blunt. I told him the course he had chosen would ruin the business by splitting the shareholders in two. There was no way most of the family would support a board that turned against my father. He listened quietly and promised to see me the following day, but next morning made it clear that there was no going back on their decision.

That was the last real conversation I ever had with Geoffrey Noakes; it was the beginning of a long period of silence. I was alienated from the rest of the board and felt the atmosphere every time I joined them for lunch or we passed in the corridor.

We faced a coup from our fellow directors and it seemed likely that I would be ousted once my father had left, leaving us with shares in a company run by people whom we felt lacked expertise and integrity. For the first time I looked at the shareholder list in detail. I knew the family held about 52% but had never contemplated family members being on different sides. I always assumed that over 50% was enough to have control – but I've since learned that you need 100% to control everything. After four generations in a fertile family the shares were split among lots of relatives, many of whom might pass in the street without recognising each other. Indeed, a few years ago I held a party for all the descendants of the company founder, William Timpson. Of the 175 invited, 135 gathered together in a marquee in our garden, a visual reminder of how diverse ownership can become in a fourth-generation family business.

My father spent a frantic 10 days gathering signatures to support our side of the argument. We rang relatives and travelled the country to meet them. I took a train to Bedford one evening to see my father's cousin, Michael, a school master who couldn't attend the family meeting held at Cranoe (my father's house in Hale) to hear the arguments and sign in support of our stance. I held 100,000 shares (about ¼ of 1%), my father had considerably more and with the backing of other family shareholders we accounted for 22% of the equity. We had three options: give up and go along with the directors' ultimatum, join battle and challenge them at an extraordinary shareholders meeting (and probably damage the company's reputation in the process) or use our shareholding to attract an outsider to bid for the company.

The group agreed that the only sensible option was to try to attract a predator. We were advised that we held enough shares to give an outsider a big enough start to expect success in a competitive bid. While we tracked down family members the clock was ticking. The ultimatum given to my father had a clear deadline. The board meeting scheduled for 20 September promised to be considerably less benign than its predecessor. It had an ominous agenda:

1. Minutes of the last meeting
2. Matters arising
3. W.A. Timpson
4. Any other business

Everyone felt the tension as four directors congregated in the executive lavatory next to the boardroom. I stood at the urinals next to Geoffrey, but we didn't say a word. He avoided my gaze by staring at the ceiling – and I did the same.

When I went into the boardroom my father was already in his chair, so I sat at the other end of the table and waited. The others came in together, looking uneasy. They had a single objective, only thinking about today, ignoring the past and with no conception of the future.

We started with the mundane minutes of the last meeting; no one made any comment, there were no matters arising, everyone stuck to their stubborn script. My father proposed an alternative to the proposition before the board. He asked for a vote of no confidence in Geoffrey and the Professor. He said they had undermined him as Chairman of the company and if allowed to take control would not have the backing of most of the family shareholders, who would, as a result, offer their shares to a likely bidder. I looked round. My fellow directors were all looking at the table pretending to listen but closing their minds to any argument that might deter them from the course that had already been set.

Geoffrey then proposed, and Professor Smith seconded, that my father should be removed. Within 90 seconds the deed was done. By a majority of six to two my father was no longer the Chairman. He made a vitriolic parting speech from the Chair, pointing out how each individual round the table had, on the one hand, taken advantage of his generosity and, on the other, put a knife in his back. In the end he stood up and challenged Geoffrey to take the Chair, which Geoffrey refused, claiming that the election of a new Chairman was a matter for another meeting.

The two losers left the boardroom together – and that is when I slammed the boardroom door. Perhaps I should have been more dignified in defeat but it wasn't a day for dignity. Within half an hour my father received a letter from Geoffrey Noakes requiring him to vacate his office within 7 days, to hand over all papers, and leave his company car (a Bristol) in the office car park. He was instructed only to enter a Timpson shop as a customer and a notice was sent out to all employees:

This is to notify you that Mr W.A. Timpson has ceased to be Chairman and an employee of the company. The Vice Chairman, Mr G.W. Noakes will deputise until a new Chairman has been appointed.

*　*　*　*　*

My great-grandfather, William Timpson, had little or no formal education. By the age of 8 he had taken a part-time job making boot laces in Rothwell, Northamptonshire. When he was 12 his father decided to send him to Manchester to work for his elder brother Charles, who was a shoe whole-saler. Life with Charles and his rather severe wife was not easy for the teenager who was determined to gain his future independence by saving every possible penny. He delivered boots by pushing an old sack barrow, but had enough energy at the end of the day to complete his education by attending night school.

One day he was late for work and his brother Charles was so angry that he beat young William with a cane. Following this incident William returned to his native Rothwell to learn shoemaking, working with a cordwainer (an old term for a master shoemaker) who opened the day by reading the bible

to his men. In those days shoemakers were considered superior – they were often people with advanced religious and
political views – and his boss was one of the intellectuals of
the town. When the old shoemaker died, William managed
his business for a time. He soon realised, however, that it
took a week to make a pair of shoes and only a few minutes
to sell them. With this in mind, at the age of 16, he gave up
shoemaking and returned to Manchester to team up with his
older sister's husband, Walter Joyce, and together they
opened a boot and shoe shop in Butler Street off Oldham
Road in Manchester.

Five years later William decided to work alone. He left his
brother-in-law and opened his own shop in Oldham Street,
not the most fashionable part of Manchester, but certainly at
that time one of the busiest. He took a big gamble by picking
a prime site and signing a lease for £200 a year – a figure
that most people thought he couldn't afford. He soon had a
threat from his next-door neighbour who tried to persuade
the landlord to give him possession of William Timpson's
shop. This tenant, without consulting the landlord, refitted
his shop. As the building was over 100 years old, rickety and
unstable, the construction work brought down some of the
shop's original walls, which gave William Timpson his first
stroke of luck. The landlord, unhappy with the damage
done, evicted the culprit, gave William the lease next door
and the chance to create a bigger shop that everyone started
to notice.

William had lots of confidence and the vision to realise that if you are doing something you might as well do it properly. A mahogany shop front and a glazed glass fascia surrounded windows lined with shoes. Inside, the shop was full of shoe boxes with the cheaper shoes hanging on hooks. The assistants wore black dresses with black satin trimmings and the owner and manager, William Timpson, wore a traditional shoemaker's apron, personally serving as many customers as he could. I would love to be taken back in time to see that shop. It mostly sold boots, as very few people wore shoes in those days. The shop stayed open late at night six days a week, plus Sunday morning before people went to church. The business was very busy, selling over 100 pairs of men's boots on a Saturday, with most customers being served by William Timpson himself. The shop seems to have been a success from the day it opened.

William kept a tight control on expenses, especially wages. His sister, who worked for him, not only served customers but also did the cleaning. William knew what he was doing. In the first year the shop made a profit of £1,000 – a stunning figure when translated into today's money – but as he didn't trust the banks and thought they were insecure, all his money went back into the business. Even when he got married he persuaded his new wife to live over the shop.

Within five years he had established a winning formula. He owned one of the best-known shoe shops in Manchester and by ploughing his profits back into property he could repeat his success many times over in other shops he acquired around the city. William had the ingredient that every new business craves for: he sold what the public wanted in shops they wanted to visit. He was creating Manchester's shoe category killer. With his passion for cost control, the business was making substantial profits. His policy of putting all his positive cash flow back into property put the business in a strong position.

There was, however, a potential problem that threatened to get in the way of his expansion. William suffered from ill health. It has been suggested that he was affected by the gas lamps that constantly created fumes inside his original shop, or maybe he was just a hypochondriac! Whatever the reason, in 1880, only 10 years after he had started the business in Oldham Street, his doctor advised him to move away from Manchester for the good of his health. He went on to have 12 children and live to the age of 79, so perhaps he was not quite as ill as he thought he was.

Following his doctor's advice he changed his lifestyle and moved to Kettering in Northamptonshire. His routine involved spending only four days a fortnight in Manchester, but despite his absence the business continued to grow. He always employed many of his relatives: one of his sisters worked in his first shop and seven of her daughters were shop assistants throughout Manchester. While he was in

Kettering, one of his brothers-in-law ran the day-to-day business in Manchester. Despite his health worries, William couldn't keep away from business and opened three shops near his home in Northamptonshire. He also started a shoe factory, which brought an added dimension to the Timpson brand. Kettering was a men's shoemaking town and William Timpson started manufacturing men's styles exclusively for his own shops.

By 1900 the business had grown to 26 branches, 20 in Greater Manchester plus shops in Northamptonshire (Kettering, Wellingborough) and Lancashire (Rochdale, Farnworth and Radcliffe). Throughout this expansion William Timpson never had an overdraft.

The employment of his relatives took on another dimension when his eldest son (also William) reached the age of 16 in 1896. The young man worked in the factory at Kettering for 2 shillings and 6 pence (= 12½p) a week, which was dramatically increased to 10 shillings (= 50p) a week when he moved to Manchester as a sales assistant in the original Oldham Street shop. He was then promoted to run the Manchester-based warehouse, and in 1903, at the age of 23, the younger William, now known as Will, took over day-to-day control of the Manchester shops. It wasn't long before Will looked outside Manchester to expand the business. He was an extrovert but for the first few years of his career he had to return to Kettering every Friday night as he was not allowed to spend weekends in Manchester (which was considered to be too wicked).

The constant commuting between Kettering and Manchester made the Timpsons regular railway passengers and it was an unwritten family rule that whenever travelling from Kettering to Manchester you took along a case of boots to save the company carriage costs.

Will Timpson was ambitious, but his father gave cautious advice. When Will wanted to expand into Lancashire his father wouldn't pay more than £150 a year in rent. As a result, his son had to travel relentlessly to find well-positioned shops on a reasonable lease. When Will took on an unusually large liability by branching out into Liverpool, father William was particularly critical and accused him of wasting past profits on his unwise ambition. Will was not deterred by this type of stern advice, however, and opened new shops in Sheffield, Blackburn, Nottingham, Leeds, Hull and Edinburgh. By 1914 he had nearly doubled the size of the chain to over 56 shops.

It wasn't just in property that Will Timpson excelled. In his early days he had been involved with the buying of ladies shoes, but when the man in charge of men's footwear was involved in a railway accident Will stepped into his place and helped to turn Timpson into a fashion leader. Will gave Timpson a distinct competitive edge by finding new styles in America and making them in the Kettering factory. The business continued to follow the simple formula established by his father – good value, straightforward methods, interesting looking shops with an attractive window display – plus the right people, dominated by family members and close friends.

In the early 1900s Will was joined in the business by three of his four brothers, Charles, Noel and Alan. Only George pursued a different route, and became a schoolmaster. While Will looked after men's shoes, Noel assumed responsibility for the ladies' trade. Being a strong administrator, Noel proved to be a good partner to his elder brother and when the founder, William Timpson, totally retired in 1919, Will took overall responsibility for the business with brother Noel as his deputy.

During the next 10 years the company opened 80 shops, nearly doubling the size of the chain to 136 branches. Will Timpson tramped round high streets looking at shops, and looking at the people to see what they were wearing. He bought individual businesses that he found through personal acquaintances or professional introduction, and very often from the odd chance remark. Establishing a chain of shops in those days was a difficult task; it involved weeks, months and years of travelling by day and night, and many hours of arguing and bargaining with landlords and agents. This was what Will Timpson loved.

The shoes Timpson made at Kettering were an important part of the shop appeal and, as the chain grew, more and more shoes were needed. The 750 pairs manufactured each week in 1896 had risen to 5,000 in 1914 and 7,000 in 1919. As this was still not enough to supply the needs of an ever-increasing chain, a large factory designed to make 17,000 pairs of shoes a week was built in North Park, Kettering, and opened in 1923.

At the beginning of 1929 the founder William Timpson died, and later that year the firm became a public company. During the difficulties of the depression in the 1930s, Timpson continued to prosper. Will Timpson was finding more opportunities as he travelled the country looking for new shops and Timpson was fast gaining the reputation of being the best shoe shop in the north of England. By 1939 there were 191 Timpson shops and, despite many losses to air raids during the war, by 1946 the number had risen to 197. By then, Will Timpson was 66 years old and his younger brother, Noel, was having a greater influence on the business. The next generation of the Timpson family was beginning to get involved – in particular, my father, who took on the purchasing of the men's shoes, and his cousins John Noakes, who was a ladies buyer, and Geoffrey Noakes, who concentrated on property and the emerging shoe repair business.

Shoe repairing had started in the early 1900s as an extra service to customers in Manchester using a central factory based in Moss Side. By 1939 there were 11 shoe repair factories scattered round the country, and after the war Noel developed several small repairing units in the cellars or attics of retail shops and also began to open some stand-alone shoe repair shops.

The business continued to grow: by 1952 there were 225 shops and more than 240 by 1955, but the chain only increased by 10 branches in the next five years. Expansion was starting to slow down. As the business was being run by a Chairman in his 70s and his brother in his 60s, the company seemed to concentrate on continuing its past success without finding ways to expand to another level.

Timpson was firmly based in the north – the market leader in all the major industrial towns – but these areas had been hit by redundancies in ship building, textiles and coal mining, and there were lots of other family shoe chains that had grown over the same period and reached a similar size. Stead & Simpson, Olivers, Saxone, Lilley & Skinner, Trueform, Manfield and Freeman Hardy and Willis were some of the best-known names among 50 or so family footwear chains of significance. The balance sheet of most of these companies was strengthened by the freehold properties they had bought during the 1930s. These property assets attracted a new player onto the high street – Charles Clore. He did what Timpson should have done. Through a series of takeovers he acquired a massive freehold property portfolio at well below market price and established a dominant national footwear chain in the process.

In 1951 Timpson made a profit of £600,000 (about £20 million in today's terms), but seven years later profits were still at the same level. The company, which had grown so rapidly, had now hit a plateau, but Will still supplied the flair and was good with people, visiting shops on a regular basis, while Noel kept tight control. Throughout this time Noel's desire to become Chairman had become more and more apparent. Eventually he got his wish in 1960 but his term of office was tragically short-lived. Within months of taking the Chair he died while gardening at his home in Cheshire. Although Noel was over 60 and Will was approaching his 80th birthday, no succession plan was clear. Only two family directors remained, my father, Anthony, and his cousin, Geoffrey.

As a stop-gap solution the Company Secretary, Gordon Akester, became Chairman; my father was his deputy as well as joint Managing Director with Geoffrey Noakes. Three years later father became the Chairman and Geoffrey the Deputy Chairman – they also continued as joint Managing Directors.

People close to the business thought that the new management structure was an unfortunate compromise. The scene was set for disharmony at a time when the company needed strong leadership. The early 1960s were good for most retailers and Timpson profits grew, but the shift in wealth from north to south took business away from the Timpson heartland. British Shoe Corporation was rapidly gaining market share and footwear started to be sold in other shops, such as Marks & Spencer, Littlewoods and British Home Stores.

Timpson did not do enough to update its property portfolio and it became progressively more difficult to find enough orders to fill the Kettering factory. Shoe buyers were distorting the range of stock to keep the factory on full production, and in 1969 Timpson had a disastrous year. The factory made a loss, a wet summer and mild winter trimmed the shoe shop sales of seasonal footwear, and the uninterrupted run of shoe repair success came to an abrupt end. Cheap imports, synthetic soles and the demise of the stiletto heel all brought bad news – the size of the shoe repair market fell by 15% for three years in succession. With all three parts of the business performing badly, the company issued a profits warning and the share price collapsed.

To kick start our recovery, Professor Roland Smith was invited in as a consultant to lead discussions and produce a corporate plan. A year later he joined the board, my father stepped down as joint Managing Director shortly afterwards, and Geoffrey Noakes became Deputy Chairman and Chief Executive.

Over the next two years Geoffrey and Professor Smith did enough to please the City, by closing the factory and making a major acquisition – 110 shops trading as Norvic. With a modest bit of massaging in the accounts, profits rose above the magic £1 million target, but the core Timpson business was continuing to lose market share and the atmosphere at Head Office was less than healthy.

By 1971 things had got so bad that the two men at the top were exchanging typewritten notes. In one, Geoffrey said, 'I do not propose to reply to the very personal remarks you made about me on Friday as I do not believe that this would be to the benefit of the company.' And in another, my father said, 'I have your letter of 9th September and again I wonder whether you realise how rudely some of your letters read?'

Geoffrey saw little value in a family business or family management. He thought birthright was a bad way to choose a leader. He planned to rebrand the shoe repair business to reduce our reliance on the Timpson name. He was stony faced at the Annual General Meeting in April 1972 when our auditor stood up in response to his appointment and said, 'I was pleased to see that another William Timpson has been christened. In many ways I think this explains the success of this company, for five generations they have been proud of the name William and, with every reason, proud of the company that bears that name.' The child he was referring to was William James Timpson, my eldest son and our current Managing Director.

That was William Timpson Limited's last Annual General Meeting.

*   *   *   *   *

If you are born into a family business you start your apprenticeship many years before going to work. I first became aware of the business when I was about 10. Every year my parents took me on a day out to Blackpool, including a trip on the tram from Fairhaven Lake to Fleetwood. My father used this opportunity to visit our shops in the area, and when I reached 10 I was allowed to join him.

His father, Will, had spent a lifetime visiting shops and listening to his employees, many of whom he knew by name. My father did the same, making sure he visited every shop every year. I followed his example and my son, James, considers shop visiting to be a fundamental part of our culture. It's the way we run the business. I'm not entirely sure why relentlessly going round the business works so well, but it does.

I officially went on the Timpson payroll in 1960. My first real job was as a shop assistant in the Timpson shoe shop in Railway Street, Altrincham, and my first real boss was Bill

Branston. I will always be grateful to Bill, who, for three months, was my manager and mentor. Despite an age difference of nearly 40 years, Bill knew how to talk to me – he taught me how look after the stock, serve customers, dress the shop window and wrap up a pair of Wellington boots using nothing but paper and string, though I never did master Bill's final flourish when he cut the string with his bare hands.

Most of my training took place on the shop floor, but every break time Bill and I went to the basement for a cup of tea. That was where he told me stories and sometimes told me off. He made the job fun and set an example. My 13 weeks with Bill sparked an enthusiasm for retailing that still burns strongly 49 years later.

Most of all I learned the importance of customer service and the influence that a sales assistant can have on a company's success. Altrincham was Bill's shop and while I was there I was part of his team. There were no computers telling us what to do; Bill ordered his own stock and recruited his own staff. There was no self-service; every customer sat down and we brought the shoes from the boxes that lined each wall. It was proper, personal service a million miles away from today's checkouts, where some shop assistants talk to their colleagues while they scan your bar code. Bill Branston's tuition has ensured that I will never take our customers for granted.

Six years later, after university, work experience at Clarks, and an eclectic cocktail of jobs at Timpson, I settled in as a buyer of ladies shoes and learned a big lesson about management. In the 1960s our office was full of status symbols: you could spot anyone's place in the pecking order by their overalls, the colour of paper they could use for memos, their designated lavatory and dining room, plus their car parking space. It was a four-minute walk from the main car park behind the warehouse to the office building, yet on the way you passed 40 spaces that were allocated strictly according to seniority. As you moved up the company management chart, your car could be parked closer to the front door.

A branch manager from the Midlands had been summoned for an interview prior to being given promotion. Being nervous he arrived early and, unaware of the car parking system, put his car in Bay 2. The space was allocated to Geoffrey Noakes who arrived in his Rolls Royce at 9 o'clock. When the manager completed his interview at 10 o'clock he found his car was blocked in by the Rolls. Geoffrey didn't leave until six and the poor manager spent the day sitting in reception. This incident occurred over 40 years ago but I've never forgotten it. It serves as a continual reminder of the dangers of arrogance – an example of exactly what big bosses should *not* do. Parking in our office today is on a first come, first served basis. If it is full when I arrive, I park by the warehouse and have a four-minute walk to the office.

In the late 1960s, when I assumed responsibility for buying ladies shoes, the business was struggling, but in 1968 I had a spectacular season. For someone with no natural fashion sense, I found buying to be fairly easy. Don't be fooled by the designers' air of mystery; fashion isn't all about flair, most of it is predictable. The best guide to this year's fashion is what you sold last year. At least two-thirds of the styles, with a slight tweak, will sell again. You can also be guided by a fairly predictable fashion cycle: toes move from pointed to round and back to pointed again, although it may take 20 years to get back to where you started. But when I was a buyer the easiest way to forecast future fashion was to go to Italy. Styles selling on the streets of Florence and Milan one year would sell in Leeds and Luton 12 months later. I spent a week in Italy every June looking at the latest fashions. I looked at what was being worn, photographed shop windows, bought some shoes and got them copied by British factories at a quarter of the price. In 1968 we spotted a trend that every other multiple missed. The winkle pickers were disappearing and it was time for big wide toes. Our new range of heavy-look shoes, called Clompers, arrived at the perfect time.

Good buying is a vital factor in the success of any shoe shop – you need the styles that customers want to buy, but buyers do better in a business that is growing. The creative team at Primark, now the darlings of the UK high street, will come under more pressure when their rapid expansion comes to an end.

By the time I became a buyer, Timpson had reached its peak of 260 branches but many of the new shops weren't bringing in much extra business. I first realised how poor our property department was when I visited our new shop at Beswick, a Manchester suburb not far from Eastlands where Manchester City now play football. At a time when the company should have been expanding into big shops in city centres, particularly in the south of England, it concentrated on small shops in northern suburbs and Beswick was the worst of them all. In this downmarket precinct with lots of empty shops, we never made a profit and had to bear the cost of security grills on every window to stop vandalism. We had lost my grandfather's flair. Instead of travelling the high street, our Property Department crunched numbers and produced appraisals. That poor approach to property acquisitions put Timpson at a severe disadvantage, but it taught me a lesson: you need to keep tramping the high street and use your gut instinct to find the prime sites that will make your business even better.

While our profits remained at around £1 million, our biggest competitor, British Shoe Corporation, went from strength to strength. With a lack of flair in the boardroom, senior management saw Professor Roland Smith as a lifeline. He organised a three-day seminar in Chester, close to home, but we had to stay in a hotel as bonding was part of his process. He preached management by objectives and Geoffrey Noakes fell for it in a big way. Geoffrey arranged a series of meetings to establish the budget for the following year, starting with the overall objective and breaking it down into individual targets. He bought a calculator for every branch manager, who now had to produce week-by-week sales for every major category. After two months of mathematics the branch detail added up precisely to the company target. At the start of the new financial year the company was poised for success, as long as everyone met their individual targets the company would have a record year. The first week was a great disappointment, most shops missed their target and the company was 8% below budget; the next week was even worse. Despite this initial setback, for the next two years the company continued to be managed by strict objectives set at Head Office. That experience taught me a lot about the limitations of consultants and central control.

The boardroom bust up in 1972 taught me my most important lesson. Ever since that meeting I have been wary of business politics. I still trust other people, but I am never surprised if someone lets me down. Most of all I understood the importance of controlling the equity – total control means having 100% of the business.

Within two weeks a buyer had been identified. The most likely purchasers were Great Universal Stores, Sears (the owners of British Shoe Corporation) or United Drapery Stores (UDS) – we chose UDS. My father met their Chairman, Bernard Lyons, who, armed with acceptances from the family, called to see Geoffrey Noakes at Wythenshawe with a bid of £1 per share, worth just under £20 million. My fellow directors suddenly realised that we had not been bluffing. Sears entered the bidding and there was a three-month take-over battle, which only ended when the Sears bid was referred to the Monopolies Commission.

In December 1972 UDS was finally the winner, buying William Timpson Limited for £28.6 million. For four months the other directors seldom spoke to me. Although I had the support of most of our workforce it was an uncomfortable experience. When my father died 26 years later, I did a lot of reminiscing and realised how much the UDS takeover had affected my approach to business. I was no longer the direc-tor of a family business with an assured future, and watching my father being undermined stuck in my memory and shaped my management style.

UDS was really another family business. The Lyons family who ran it were sympathetic to my plight, found me a job elsewhere in the group. I was transferred to Leeds and given the task of introducing footwear into the John Collier tailor-ing shops. It wasn't much of a job – they only wanted shoes in an initial 20 shops and at best we were selling 200 pairs a week, which was hardly worth the two hour daily trip to Leeds at a time before the M62 had been built.

I was soon spending most of my time gardening, playing golf and contemplating my future. After three months of semi-retirement at the age of 29, I was itching to find something more interesting to do and UDS suggested a job in London buying shoes for one of their department stores. I went for an interview, determined to hand in my resignation with no plans other than a vague thought of opening a shoe shop of my own. In the end, however, I was offered an entirely different job. Ten days before, UDS had parted company with the entire management team of a small chain of shops based in Liverpool. The company – called Swears & Wells – had 60 shops, half of which were trading as Suede Centre, selling fur coats and leather clothing. Sales had collapsed and it was making a loss. 'You live near Liverpool,' said Bernard Lyons, UDS Chairman. 'Go over there and look after the company for a few weeks and see what you can do.' The following Monday morning I arrived at the Swears & Wells Head Office to find that all that was left in their executive suite was the Personnel Director and a large tank full of tropical fish. Sales for the previous week were less than half of last year's level, and the 60 shops had only managed to take £25,000 between them.

Swears & Wells was a really lucky break. It was the perfect training course for a Chief Executive. I spent 10 days travelling round to find out what was going on, and I soon discovered that selling fur and leather was all about price – people like to buy a bargain. 'We would take a lot more money', said the manager of Oxford Circus when I made my first visit, 'if only I could bargain with customers. Foreign visitors are only satisfied when they can do a deal. The previous management wouldn't let me haggle so I just stuck to their rules. The current lousy turnover shows how much business we are losing.' I told the managers in both Oxford Street shops that they could drop prices by up to 15% and launched a July sale in the rest of the chain. Within two weeks turnover was beating last year.

Swears & Wells was such a small part of UDS that no one bothered me. I was left in Liverpool to get on with it. Within three weeks I had another piece of luck – the shop in New Street, Birmingham, caught fire. Margaret Broadley, the Personnel Director, who I had first encountered in the barren office with the tropical fish, rang me on a Friday morning to give me the bad news. 'The shop is still standing,' she said, 'but all the stock is smoke damaged, we have started to clear it up, with luck the shop should open again on Monday.' I remembered the benefits of a fire sale in our shoe shop in Wilmslow two years earlier and I made my first executive decision, 'Keep it shut,' I said, 'don't open again until next Friday.' We plastered the window with big posters announcing *Fire Sale Starts Friday 10.00 a.m.*', by which time a large queue had formed. In two days we took more money than the shop had taken in the previous 20 weeks. The big sales figure from Birmingham had a significant effect on our total sales for the week, giving Swears & Wells the highest percentage increase of any part of UDS. Pleased with my success, the Lyons told me I could keep the job, and I stayed there for the next two years.

I learned a lot about the importance of visiting shops and worked out that the best way to run a business is to persuade, not to dictate. I learned the benefits that come from getting to know your colleagues and looking after them. Most of all I discovered how much your own personal management style can influence success. I also learned that whenever you are offered a golden opportunity, grab it straight away.

I'd been in the job just under two years when my lucky break at Swears & Wells turned into a fairy story. One Monday morning I was sitting at my desk in Bold Street, Liverpool, when Stuart Lyons rang to ask whether I would like to return to Timpson as Managing Director. It was a magic moment – a dream come true, and the following week I went to London to start planning my new job at Timpson. On Wilmslow Station waiting for the Pullman I spotted Geoffrey Noakes further down the platform. This would be his last visit to UDS.

Despite the experience at Swears & Wells I still had a lot to learn before I was equipped to run a business that, in those days, had 500 shops. I lived on adrenalin, learned by experience and profits steadily improved during the first 12 months. Then we hit the summer of 1976. Initially the heat wave helped, clearing out all the sandals and producing some extremely good results in July. But the blue skies continued well into the autumn, and by the time Harold Wilson had appointed Denis Howell as Minister for Drought the sales of our autumn merchandise were suffering dramatically. Denis Howell did the trick; within 10 days of his appointment it poured with rain, but it was too late to save our autumn business and by that time I, for the first time in my life, was suffering from stress. Within weeks I had turned from a confident optimist to a nervous pessimist. It was a big lesson: arrogance and complacency won't last forever. It's always best to keep your feet on the ground.

As well as starting to understand how to run multiple shops, I also learned about groupmanship. Controlling a subsidiary has different priorities from running your own business; you need to learn the groupmanship game – how to avoid criticism and get the funds needed for investment. The trick is to avoid being the worst performing company in the group – if possible keep out of the bottom two. Fortunately at UDS there was always another business doing worse than we were, indeed many UDS companies did so badly that they made a loss and some were closed down. In the space of seven years I saw UDS close John Myers, mail order, Grange Furnishing in Scotland, Alexandre and Claude Alexander the tailoring shops, a number of department stores including Whiteley's of Bayswater, and the fashion chain Van Allen, which the group had only purchased two years earlier. This consistent record of failure was good for Timpson while it lasted, but it could not last forever. When the core retail chains of John Collier and Richard Shops also started to make losses, it was clear that UDS was about to lose its independence.

One summer evening in 1982, Alex and I accepted an invitation to a charity dinner. Our party included several unfamiliar faces, and Alex sat next to one of them, Roger Lane-Smith. Roger was the senior partner of a small but high-profile legal firm in Manchester and he was always on the lookout for the next opportunity. He talked to Alex about my job and the possibilities of buying our business. Alex, attracted by his enthusiasm, saw the chance of a complete change in our future fortune, and Roger made an appointment to see me the following week.

My first concern was confidentiality. I had a secure position with UDS, but if the Lyons family discovered that I was plotting to buy the business, I could lose my job. But Alex put my mind at rest, 'I'm just telling you it will work out,' she said. She had an intuitive conviction that Roger held the key to our future. I didn't need much persuading, and as I wasn't designed for a safe but humdrum management job, an inward ambition was aroused by the excitement in prospect.

My next year was dominated by something I'd never heard of before – a Management Buyout. It seemed like a fantasy: I had no money, just a house and a big mortgage, so I didn't see how we could buy a £3 million profit company with £30 million worth of property assets. When I met the directors of the venture capital firm, Candover, I started to understand. But my continuing faith in the deal came from Alex, who, every step of the way, would reassure me: 'I'm telling you it will work.' And of course it did. Since then I've been much more inclined to follow my gut reaction and always trust Alex's judgement. It's never wise to make a decision entirely on the basis of figures from the finance department and reports from your team. Always leave room for flair and intuition.

It only took a year for the fairytale to turn into a nightmare. It had been a dream come true, as the company I thought had disappeared forever was suddenly a family business once more. I was walking on air hardly able to believe what had happened. When I woke from the dream, I discovered that independent life was not quite as good as expected. Our business plan expected the company to go from strength to strength and float on the Stock Exchange with all of us – including employees, investors and directors – enjoying the experience, but it didn't happen. The buyout put me under pressure. Having achieved the dream of buying back the family business, I had to make it successful. Not only did I need to satisfy the demands of my management shareholders, the venture capitalists and the clearing bank, who all expected to see success, but I had also to live up to my own expectations and could not afford to fail.

For 12 months the company traded fairly well but soon sales stagnated and profits started to fall. High rents, increased competition and changes in fashion made business difficult. Our high gearing put me under pressure and I made a few bad decisions that made matters worse. Throughout 1984 we were overstocked; we had bought too many boots. Good buying is critical to a fashion business, but even good buyers can have a bad season.

The shoe repair business was also having a difficult time. Suddenly it faced a new threat – trainers. In five years 25% of the shoe market had switched to footwear that was never repaired. At the same time imports forced down the price of new shoes, and shoe repairers were under more pressure than ever before, particularly in the northern towns and suburbs where our core business was based. Then a lifeline came out of the blue.

During my work experience in 1961, the six weeks I spent in a shoe repair factory were not covered in glory. Frankly, I was so bad that after a week I was moved from the technical side to look after customers. But I knew more about shoe repairs than Kit Green, a marketing manager from the days before UDS, who had just returned to Timpson. Despite our lack of expertise it was a meeting between us, two total amateurs, that started the major change which was to give us our critical edge. At that time I was spending my life in meetings, not just the formal sort that have agendas and minutes but long discussions that got nowhere, talking endlessly round our major problems without finding a solution.

That meeting with Kit was different, we came up with an idea and decided to try it. To compensate for the loss of shoe repair sales, the shops sold a wide range of merchandise, much of it at a low margin. We knew that key cutting was our highest margin business: every £1 of merchandise sales earned a margin of 27 pence, but each £1 of key cutting brought in 65 pence. If we could swap merchandise sales for key cutting we would make more money. We chose two shops, Leicester and Gloucester, threw out all the hosiery, shopping baskets and wickerware and filled a big wall with keys. It worked. Key sales immediately doubled and doubled again; we had made a remarkable difference to profits and, in the process, had become expert key-cutters. After the initial success we put the big key board into another 10 shops, then another 10, and within four years we'd changed every shop. In 1986 our key-cutting turnover was under £500,000 – it is now approaching £40 million. You don't make any money by simply talking about problems. It's the new ideas that develop the business and ideas don't have a chance of working unless you try them.

The big key board helped our shoe repair business but the shoe shops still suffered. Under pressure to see our profits rise I was persuaded to make some sweeping changes, and two years after the buyout I became Chairman, handing over executive responsibility to a new management team recruited from the Burton Group. The change in management style was dramatic and Timpson did not take kindly to the difference. The employees felt that I had exchanged a wealth of experience for expensive executives who knew nothing about the shoe business. The new team worked very long hours, sales got even worse and the business was heading towards a loss.

Just in time I learned the importance of getting the thinking straight and took a hard look at the future of our shoe shops. The shops faced a number of problems: it was a time of inflation, but shoe prices were not increasing, and cheap imports were bringing prices down. For years there had been far too many specialist shoe shops on the high street and now other shops were selling shoes, such as Marks & Spencer, Littlewoods and clothing chains like Burtons and C&A. Training shoes brought competition from specialist sports shops and fashion didn't help, as the wide variety of styles demanded by the public called for higher stocks. We had a poor stock turn and needed big shops to accommodate all the shoes; this meant high rents for the prime positions we required but we could not afford them.

Three years after the buyout I was facing failure; but, fortunately, I was the first to realise that the whole of shoe retailing was heading for disaster. When I couldn't financially justify opening another shoe shop it was clearly time to sell.

I put my thoughts down on paper. At the top of the sheet I wrote 'Timpson Shoe Shops – The Future' and made two columns: one headed 'Against' and the other 'For'. Once I had filled the 'Against' column with bad news, the simple question was: Why should we continue?

Timpson Shoe Shops - The Future

Against	*For*
Cheap shoes	Strong brand
Trainers	Family tradition
British Shoe Corporation	
Mail order	
High rents	
Shopfitting costs	
Cut price competition	
Shoe fashion less predictable	
M&S/BHS selling shoes	
Concessions	
Low stock turn	
Wage inflation	
High markdowns	

Conclusion: We can't open another new shop.

The only reason to continue was personal pride. It took three months to break my emotional ties sufficiently to take the decision and put the shoe shops up for sale, and it took another eight months to sell them.

It took me too long to come to terms with the facts. If I'd been more detached and more decisive I would have got a much higher price. In the end we were probably lucky to find a buyer like George Oliver, a 350 shop shoe multiple based in Leicester with its stores mainly in the Midlands, the southwest of England, and Wales. We were a perfect fit and agreed terms at £15 million. We devised a scheme that not only took us out of shoe retailing but retained control of our shoe repair shops. I didn't want to retire at 44 and Alex certainly didn't want me to be hanging around the house.

The shoe repair shops were making profits of £450,000 and as I still wanted to run a business, Timpson Shoe Repairs gave me that opportunity. Selling the shoe shops was the hardest and probably the best decision of my life, which for me was only made possible by writing lists. I think the most useful tools for a Chief Executive are a pen and an A4 pad.

It took six months to recover from the trauma of selling the shoe shops, but I soon realised that I had not only changed the business, I had also changed my lifestyle. For the first time in my life I had cash in the bank and could move to a large house with a small mortgage. I started to play tennis and golf during the week and still had time for a regular day off with Alex.

The shorter my working week, the better the business seemed to do – a workaholic Chief Executive doesn't necessarily make a business more profitable. The company only had four shareholders: I held the majority stake, followed by Peter Cookson my Finance Director, Mike Williams the Property Director and Roger Lane-Smith. The pressures of shoe retailing had left little time for anything else, so I had never been closely involved in shoe repairs, and although I couldn't repair a shoe, I found the business fascinating. We were soon looking for ways to expand, and within months we made our first acquisition – Shoetech, a 12-branch chain of shoe repair shops based in the south and Midlands but owned by two entrepreneurs living in Jersey. We bought the company for shares that gave the owners, John Stratford and Chris Fowler, 18% of our equity and seats on the board. Our long-term aim was to float, so we saw a paper purchase as the cheapest way to grow while keeping the company in credit at the bank.

We intended to be another niche retailer following in the footsteps of Sock Shop, Tie Rack and Body Shop, who had recently come to the market at P/E ratios* between 35 and 50. The Shoetech purchase was completed in October 1987, and as the stock market collapsed four days later we were lucky to have done the deal. We appointed a

---

*Price/Earnings ratio: The relationship between the share price and the dividend per share.

stockbroker to organise the float but never wrote the prospectus; we were the niche retailer that never came to market.

Alex stopped my ambitions: she told me I was mad. When everyone else was rushing to the market, Alex told me to keep clear. She saw the benefits of a private business and the threat of city analysts and demanding shareholders. Once my intentions became clear, the Jersey-based shareholders turned against me. Despite an improvement in profits, they said I was incompetent and wrote a long letter listing my faults. They had a justified grievance. When we bought their business we had agreed to float, and I had broken that promise. The end solution was to buy out their shareholding. Although their 12 shops cost over £1 million – which, at more than £80,000 per shop, made Shoetech our most expensive purchase – 11 of the 12 shops still survive today and have repaid the £1 million four times over.

I then encountered criticism from closer at home. Mike Williams and Peter Cookson were minority shareholders and wanted the protection of a shareholder's agreement. They had a good point, so I agreed that they could sell me their shareholding on a P/E of 10 at any time during the next five years, after which I had the option to buy their shares on the same multiple. The company did well for three years: we acquired three businesses, grew to 225 shops and bought a 26% stake in our next largest competitor, Automagic.

Everything was fine until another recession hit the high street and slim heels went out of fashion. In 1991 profits fell from £1.8 million to £1.3 million and I discovered that I was being increasingly criticised by my fellow directors. I resisted their calls for a cost-cutting campaign, being convinced from my branch visits that our competitors' trade was even worse. One Friday afternoon Peter Cookson came to my office stating that he was immediately going to invoke our agreement in respect of half of his 20% shareholding. The formula, based on the record profits of the previous year, made half his stake worth £1 million. Mike Williams saw me the following Monday, stating that he wanted to cash in all his shares. That single weekend had swallowed up all my personal assets and put me on the other side of the negotiating table from my two main directors and shareholders.

Yet again, Alex provided the right instinctive advice and we chose the most expensive solution. I offered to buy the 35% of shares I did not own, but had to find £3.5 million within three weeks. We raided the company cash flow, sold all my investments, used most of my spare cash and still needed to take a £1 million mortgage on our house. I ended five years of personal financial security, but it was well worth it as I now own 100% of the business.

There was no public announcement and I said nothing to the people in the company, but the business had changed. As sole owner I started to manage in a different way.

Overnight, it was much more my business, where staff and customers were seen as the main asset, and I took a longer-term view of our future fortunes.

Until 1987 most of my time had been concentrated on the retail shoe shops. It took me some time to understand how we could improve our shoe repair service shops, and it was several years before I understood the importance of training. I saw the light during another of those chance conversations, this time with Mike Donoghue who was then product manager for our shoe repair service. I asked him how we set our quality standards. 'We aim to produce a good commercial job,' he said, 'but we don't go into detail.' I suddenly realised the folly of training people without having a standard to aim for. 'Stay there,' I said to Mike, 'I'll be back in 15 minutes.' I shot off in the car round to our local garden centre where I bought four illustrated gardening books written by Dr. D.G. Hessayan. 'That's what we need,' I said to Mike when I returned. 'Training manuals in pictures rather than words – guidelines that show our people exactly how they can produce that good commercial job.'

Following that conversation I wrote our first training manuals. This was a comprehensive series of guides covering everything we do, which dramatically changed our approach to training. Peter Harris, our training manager, seized the opportunity with enthusiasm, and training now plays a central part in our success.

In 1997 we introduced skill levels and skill tests to monitor standards and we linked skill levels to our bonus scheme. Connecting training with pay made a big difference. Something new has been added to Timpson training every year since the first manual was written in 1996. Before I had that meeting with Mike I saw training as another piece of administration and red tape. Our conversation turned me into a top training enthusiast: our pictorial manuals and skills-based testing system cost us about £3 million a year – it is some of the best money we have ever spent.

Despite a fairly hostile trading environment in the early 1990s, the business made progress and was doing much better than its major competitors – so much so that in 1995 we bought the 110-shop Automagic chain from the receiver. This made us the biggest turnover shoe repair chain in the UK. Our major competitor was Mr Minit, part of a worldwide organisation. Minit UK had more shops than we had, but their worldwide formula did not work too well in Britain. We were steadily increasing our market share.

In 1997 Mr Minit Worldwide was bought by the Swiss Bank UBS. We had already had meetings with the Minit founder, Donald Hillsdon-Ryan, but he never saw us as a serious buyer for his UK business. Shortly after the purchase of UBS, I went to see Ian Siddall, who was in charge of Minit, to propose buying the UK business, but my offer was rejected. 'We are experts at buying family businesses and putting in professional management,' he said. 'You could be next on my list.'

Suddenly, I realised we could be facing serious competition. UBS had vast sums of money that could be used to open shops next door to us, poach our staff and aggressively compete on price. I decided the only way we could defend our business was by giving customers a good-quality job and the best possible service. Our success, therefore, depended on how branch colleagues dealt with customers, and I realised for the first time that the way to provide great personal service was to give branch staff total authority and trust them to get on with it. It was this thought that led to the concept of 'Upside Down Management' which, for the last 10 years, has set our management style and been a major reason behind our success.

There are several examples of very successful family businesses: Clarks, Specsavers, Sainsbury and Marks & Spencer all owe their development to a strong family commitment. Although people talk of clogs to clogs in three generations, I am generation No. 4 and my fifth generation son, James, is well established as our Managing Director.

All our five children had a spell working in our branches between school and university, but only James opted for a career in our business. At 14 James was spending school holidays working in our shops in Northwich and Chester.

Between school and university he was trained as a shoe repairer by a master craftsman, Stan Knagg in Kirkby near Liverpool. When he graduated from Durham, he decided to get experience elsewhere. As 1993 was not a good year to go job hunting, most of his applications were rejected and he failed two interviews. Thinking that his name was a disadvantage, we decided to use a different approach and sent a 'James on free trial' offer in the form of an advert to a number of leading employers. James got a job with Johnson's Apparelmaster working as a salesman in the north-east.

He made a permanent move to Timpson two years later and it soon became clear that he had a mind of his own and a thirst for new ideas. James launched us into the world of watch repairs, which has since become a multi-million pound business. But not everything he touched turned to gold. He invented citycobbler.com, the website that offered an instant shoe repair service at your office desk: e-mail our motorcyclist and he'll come with a pair of slippers for you to wear while your shoes are repaired and returned within the hour. Within days of the launch the motorcyclist fractured his shoulder falling off his bike and the scheme was an instant failure.

It's not easy being born with a silver spoon in your mouth and some people thought James was far too young to become the Managing Director (he was 31, slightly older than I was when I got the same job). Six years later he is well established. I'm often asked, 'How do you make it work between father and son?'

It could be a problem being married to your Managing Director's mother, but it has worked very well for me. James and I talk about everything and anything to do with the business. I'm delighted to say he still asks for my advice. 'What happened the last time the Government increased VAT?' 'Did we ever have a shop in Stalybridge?' 'How did you handle inflation when it went up to 25%?' During this constant debate we seldom disagree. On the rare occasions that we have a different point of view, he wins (he's like his mother).

When James took on the job he made it crystal clear that he wasn't looking for a caretaker role; he wasn't there to babysit his father's project. 'I know people think you've already done it,' he told me, 'but I want to achieve my own goals, I want to put my own stamp on the business.' It's worked; in the last six years we've seen a five-fold increase in our profits, spurred on by his determination to expand the business by introducing new ideas. At the same time, James has been frugal (a trait not inherited from his mother), consistently keeping a tight control on costs. He has, however, inherited his mother's social conscience, which has driven him to provide free holiday homes for our colleagues and develop a ground-breaking training scheme which is helping ex-offenders to join our workforce.

For James and me, our day-to-day job has been a perfect business school. We don't go on business courses, we don't use management consultants – we learn the big lessons by going about our business and listening to our colleagues.

Chapter Two

UPSIDE DOWN MANAGEMENT

I never thought that one decision could bring so much improvement, but the development of Upside Down Management has brought a bonanza of benefits. Upside Down Management is not a process, it is a culture. Here, I want to describe how our kind of delegation has worked and evolved in practice.

Fundamentally, Upside Down Management gives power to the people in the front line who meet customers and make the money – everyone else is there to help. These are the basic principles:

1. All colleagues have the freedom to do their jobs the way they choose.
2. Every boss's job is to help his or her team.
3. No KPIs, no boxes to tick.
4. Bosses don't issue orders.
5. Head Office is a helpline – it does not run the day-to-day business.

In 1997 when I decided to change the way we ran our business our turnover was £45 million and profits were £2.7 million. Today our takings are over £150 million and trading profits have reached £15 million. Other basic statistics also show a dramatic improvement – our percentage of overheads has gone down, as has labour turnover. But the main advantage of Upside Down Management is not seen in our Management Accounts. Customer service has improved dramatically, which was always our main objective. We still receive complaints but now we get many more compliments. I'm constantly amazed by the number of customers who take the trouble to pick up a pen simply to tell us about the good service they received in their local store.

As well as better service, I now also see better salesmanship and happier customers, and I'm happier too. Running the business has become much less stressful. We are attracting higher quality recruits and progress is no longer hampered by drongos (our name for useless underperformers). There is much more of a buzz about the business, with hardly a hint of 'them and us' between management and colleagues. I find that work is now a lot more fun. It is definitely easier to run an upside down business.

You probably think I've got things out of proportion. Surely I am exaggerating to claim so many benefits from one simple change.

In 2009 I was involved in a programme on Radio 4 with the presenter Peter Day. We went round some shops together to check out how Upside Down Management works in practice. He got a very positive response, and several customers talked to our branch colleagues about the programme and some sent me personal e-mails. Here are the first three I received:

'Listening to you on Radio 4's In Business has prompted me to let you know of an outstanding thing a member of your staff did last Friday. My sole needed restitching, when I came to collect the boot he showed me the work then said, "Please just put £1 in our *ChildLine* box." I was staggered that the (admittedly small) job was done free of charge. Having heard the details of your bonus scheme on the programme, I am now even more staggered that the shop staff were willing to give up their 15% commission on my repair. I thought I would let you know how much I appreciate the service.'

Another listener e-mailed to say:

'I was fascinated by the programme on Radio 4 about how you run your business. What a coincidence that only an hour before I'd been singing the praises of your website. I ordered three jars of shoe cream last night and they were delivered at 10 a.m. this morning. What a fantastic service.'

And the third e-mail said:

> 'I'm just writing to let someone know that listening to the Radio 4 programme about how the company is run was inspiring. Taking out EPOS (electronic point of sale) tills because they get in the way of shop people running their business was a great example. Well done everybody.'

Colleagues who have joined us in the last few years think that every other business is run like ours and wonder why other people believe our style of management is so revolutionary. But if you listen to what our long-service colleagues say, you start to understand what has made the difference.

Here are some comments I have heard while visiting our shops during the last two years:

Barbara Mead, who now runs our shop in Durham, told me:

> 'I've seen a lot of changes during 24 years. In the old days we were told to keep our heads down, but now I'm free to do what I want. I can use my ideas to run the branch; if I have any problems I just ring Andy, my area manager. Some friends who work for other companies think it's odd that we can talk directly to senior management like you and James, but it seems natural at Timpson. We develop our business by looking after

customers, not by sticking to rules laid down by Head Office. I like the way the business takes note of us in the shops. You've made it easier for us to make money out of the weekly bonus.'

Fran Donaghy, an area development manager in Scotland, joined us from Mr Minit whose culture was completely different. For him it was a dramatic change:

'It's weird at first,' he observed, 'but it works. It brings a very relaxed attitude and proves you don't need strict discipline. Although you allow people to do what they want, all Timpson shops look the same and our house-keeping is better than other repairers.'

Upside Down Management would not have worked if the concept hadn't been fully embraced and enthusiastically developed by our area management team, which is headed by Perry Watkins. While we were out visiting shops, Perry made an interesting observation:

'I like the way we develop new projects, gradually spreading ideas through the business by building up confidence. It's not a case of tablets of stone being handed down by senior management, it's more a consensus that only lets us pursue things that create success. Although someone decides on the final plan, no big boss takes the credit. People know that the company belongs to you and James but they make decisions as if it were their own money – that's in sharp contrast to places where people protect their power base and pursue promotion. They push their own decisions at the expense of the corporate good.'

Karina, a key member of our finance team, put it another way:

'I like the people I work with and I'm allowed to be me. Most of all I feel I've played a part in making this business what it is. You don't make decisions in an ivory tower, you listen to what people say. It is refreshing to see us revisit decisions, if it doesn't work we change it, even if it does work you still ask, "Can it be done better?" '

When he joined us in January 2004 our Finance Director, Paresh Majithia, had to adapt to a completely different company culture:

'It's difficult to describe to other people, but it is definitely different at Timpson. You allow people to get on with it; as James says, "If you can take more money by painting your shop pink, that's fine by me." Our management team is almost entirely home-grown. We have trained raw recruits to become experts. Instead of having loads of KPIs like some companies, we keep the targets simple – daily cash, weekly turnover and monthly profit, and although I was brought up with budgets I can see why you compare everything with last year. Communication is better than in a lot of businesses, producing a company newsletter week after week for many years must have had a huge impact. But despite our success you still have the ability to change your mind. I don't find people making excuses or covering their backs; our flexibility is worth a lot. It is different being part of a private business that takes a long-term view.'

Comments from our colleagues give me even more confidence than the figures in our management accounts. When I hear people in our shops saying that they are more relaxed, feel valued, are not just numbers on the personnel records, and they like the freedom they've been given, I know that they're going to be much better at serving customers than other shops whose staff have to follow company rules.

One of our biggest challenges is to get area teams to treat their people the way we want. So it was good to hear area manager, Darren Brown, tell me, 'You and James treat me as if we're on the same level. I like that, so I treat everyone in my area in the same way.'

As another area manager said, 'Upside Down Management isn't for wimps, it's for managers with the courage to give people their freedom.'

It took 10 years to ingrain this new way of working into our culture. My deepest thinking colleagues realise that this is a never-ending project. As Perry Watkins said, 'We always live on a tightrope – it wouldn't take long for the magic dust to disappear.'

Rosemary, who looks after our pension scheme, put it another way: 'Please don't change things; as long as you keep the business as relaxed as it is now we will never be frightened to tell you about any problems. As we get bigger we must retain our management style. It would be a disaster to turn into a target driven company run by committees who take away individual freedom. I want you to keep it simple. When you visit branches or come round the office you make people feel they are worthwhile. There is no doubt that our style of management has brought tremendous benefits. The biggest task you face is to ensure that we don't get derailed by professional managers who think they know better.'

I am embarrassed that it took me 22 years as a Chief Executive before I found the secret behind good personal customer service. But it's true. I didn't discover Upside Down Management until I met Ian Siddall at UBS. I remember that morning in vivid detail, waiting in their vast entrance hall well beyond the time scheduled for our appointment, and drinking tea in a waiting room for a further 15 minutes while I waited for Mr Siddall to finish a previous meeting. I had a simple mission – I wanted to see whether they would sell us their UK shops, but as soon as he told me he was an expert at buying family businesses and turning them round by putting in professional management, I knew I was wasting my time. But the meeting had not been wasted. Far from it. I learned that we faced a new threat, a competitor with more money than I could possibly imagine, who was well placed to inflict major damage on our business. He could have opened shops next door, bribed our best people to jump ship and undercut our prices. To survive we had to be good at shoe repairing and key cutting, engraving and watch repairs and be great at looking after customers.

Most multiple retailers claim to give customer care a high priority. They set out rules designed to make sure that staff are polite to customers and sell at the same time. Every assistant is expected to serve customers properly by conforming to the company standard. I made the same mistake. In the 1970s I wrote my '10 Golden Rules of Service' to tell our shoe shop assistants exactly what to do. It didn't really work. No rule can cater for the unexpected, true personal service means giving what individual customers want, not what the company says they need. Anyone can deal with the 90% of customers who come up to expectations. Service disasters occur when an organisation fails to have the flexibility to deal with the 10% who need something special.

All this was running through my mind the night after I'd met Ian Siddall. Then I remembered a book I'd read about a department store chain in the USA – *The Nordstrom Way* – in which I saw a management chart that was upside down. They went to extraordinary lengths to give individual sales people the freedom to bring in the extra sale. The book describes how it worked, with some spectacular stories of heroic salesmanship that went well beyond the call of duty.

When I woke the next morning I was totally convinced. The way to beat the threat from Mr Minit was to provide our people with the freedom to give great service. I was already starting to call it Upside Down Management, and I thought the idea was so obvious that everyone would get it straight away – but I was wrong. I put an upside down chart on the front of our weekly newsletter and wrote a letter to everyone explaining my new philosophy, but nothing changed. No one believed I meant it. What I proposed was so contrary to the way a normal business is managed that they simply didn't trust me. I discovered that lots of people like rules; they don't want the freedom to make up their own mind. The rules give a degree of comfort, providing something to complain about and something or someone else to blame.

After a time I realised that just telling people that they've got freedom to act was not good enough. I had to give them examples of what that freedom meant, so I stuck a notice up in every branch:

> *The staff in this shop have my total authority*
> *to do whatever they can to give you amazing service.*

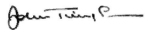

I announced that everyone, including our latest recruit, could spend up to £500 to settle a complaint without getting permission from anyone else. I also said that our price list should be treated as a guide, if anyone had a good reason to charge a lower, or sometimes a higher price, that's what they should do. I started to see a difference. Some colleagues began doing deals by bargaining with customers and the number of complaints referred to our area managers dropped dramatically. But the change in attitude varied from one shop to another. We were about to discover the big part that personality plays in Upside Down Management – it only works with the right people.

Most of our recruitment is done by area managers who each look after about 30 shops. They were looking for shoe repairers and key cutters, which you might think was logical, but they should have been looking for personalities. You can teach a positive personality to repair shoes, but you can't put personality into a grumpy cobbler. This was the first of many lessons learned by adopting Upside Down Management;

our change in style went far beyond its original focus on customer care. We were soon starting to turn the whole of our organisation upside down, giving individuals freedom to use their initiative throughout the management structure.

There is plenty of evidence that rules get in the way of personal service. We are surrounded by inflexible people who think life is all about regulation. We all have our own, personal stories to tell of times when rude, rule bound, customer service has driven us mad.

Once I was thwarted by a solicitor. My son, Oliver, needed representation following a driving offence. Due to an inability to control his own cash, Oliver was penniless, so I paid the legal fees. I sent a deposit of £1,000, but as the final cost was less than expected, the refund cheque for £323.65 was made out to Oliver. I asked for the cheque to be made payable to me instead. 'Not possible,' said the accounts manager, 'our regulations state that all payments must be to the named client, and that's your son.' 'But it's my money,' I pleaded. 'Sorry, we can't break rules, it's a money laundering guideline. I suggest your son writes a letter authorising us to pay you.' 'Not so easy,' I said, 'he's gone away. Can't you possibly use some common sense?' To which she actually replied, 'It's more than my job's worth.'

In 1999 as we approached the millennium, my wife, Alex, believed that everything was about to be in short supply, as a result of chaos from the feared Y2K computer meltdown.

I went to a pet supermarket to buy a bulk quantity of pet food – enough to last our two dogs and a cat for months. I needed a trolley, which required a £1 coin to release it. I didn't have a £1 coin, so I went to the checkout girl.

'Could you give me five £1 coins for a £5 note please?'
'Can't do that, luv,' she said, 'not allowed in the till without the supervisor.'
'Where can I find the supervisor?'
'She's on a break,'
'But,' I said patiently, 'I need a trolley to buy some of your pet food and I haven't got a £1 coin.'
'Have to wait,' she said.

I spotted the supervisor at the back of the store. 'Give me two minutes,' she said with a smile and solved my problem.

Many managers seem particularly paranoid when it comes to complaints, insisting that even the smallest problem is handled by higher authority. In Max Spielmann, a chain of shops we bought in December 2008, every complaint was referred to an area manager, who, in turn, had to get authority from the complaints department at Wishaw, near Glasgow, before giving the customer any compensation. This took time. Few complaints were settled in less than a fortnight and many took more than a month. The Complaints Department was constantly being pestered for decisions, keeping their team of 15 people very busy. After acquiring

Max Spielmann we immediately gave branch colleagues the authority to settle complaints just as we do in Timpson. We didn't need anyone extra at Timpson House to replace the 15 people in Wishaw.

Fundamentally, these problems result from a lack of delegation, but even a basic bit of Upside Down Management won't work if computers get in the way, as I discovered when I tried to buy a sausage roll at a bakery in Gosport.

'Can I have a small sausage roll please?'
'Can't sell you that,' said the woman behind the counter. 'They are three for £1.'
'I only want one.'
'The computer will only sell three.'
'What if I made you an offer?'
'No point, it wouldn't go through the till.'

I had a similar problem at a hotel in Edinburgh, where I thought I'd had a lucky break. The pleasant waitress kindly mentioned that we were in happy hour with two drinks available for the price of one.

'Great,' I replied, 'Please bring two pints – I'll take the second in for dinner.'
'No problem,' she smiled, but returned with only one glass.
'Sorry,' she said, 'the computer says it's seven o'clock – happy hour is over.'

Computer-controlled rules are cropping up all over the place. One Sunday I was sent to purchase a PlayStation 2 for my grandchildren. The children chose the pack they wanted and we stood in line next to a bluntly worded notice: 'Customer Abuse – customers giving verbal abuse to our dedicated staff will be ejected and the police will be informed.' Could the painfully slow service have pushed previous customers to the limit?

When it was our turn to be served there was a problem. The pack included two free games.

> 'You must choose,' said the sales assistant turning to me. Of the four games on offer two were rated certificate 18 and one was unavailable.
> 'But this is for my grandchildren,' I said, 'couldn't I choose a different game?'
> 'No,' he replied impatiently, 'it's against our rules.'
> He suggested a solution: 'We do part exchange. You could swap one of the "18s" for another game.'

He chose a second-hand disc on sale for £15 in exchange for the £34.95 game I had bought. I was £20 down on the deal.

> 'I need your name and postcode,' he said.
> 'Do I have to?' I asked.
> 'It's the rule,' he said.

'But,' I protested, realising they wanted my details in case the DVD was stolen, 'I haven't even touched it; it's your game and it's still in your shop.'

Sadly I lost the will to argue further, and I couldn't disappoint my grandchildren.

Shoe repairers have fallen into the same trap. The EPOS tills at Mr Minit kept everyone in a strait jacket. They were programmed remotely from Head Office and everyone had to do as they were told. Branch manager Paul Masters, who at one time worked for Minit, told me of the trouble he encountered one Monday morning with his first key-cutting customer. When he rang the sale through the till, he discovered that Head Office had changed the prices. Instead of £4, the cylinder key was now £4.62 – an unannounced experiment by Head Office designed to increase the margin which, within weeks, sent sales down by 25%.

These examples of bad customer service explain why we have removed EPOS from all the shops we have acquired in the last 15 years. These expensive terminals, modems and PCs have been replaced by a simple contraption that isn't much more than an adding machine. Computers can do a lot of harm by treading on tradition, but their biggest crime is the way they kill initiative. Strategists presume that all business intelligence resides at Head Office – an egocentric stance that puts a block on the best source of ideas.

Statisticians seldom listen to those who understand the business best – the people who serve the customers. We have been seduced by technology – embarrassed into embracing the new world of computer control. Don't let IT take charge. Make sure that people still run the business.

I have good news for members of the Customer Care Preservation Society – all is not lost. Every week I receive reports of good and often amazing service at Timpson. Here are two examples:

Ashley in Pontypridd saved a bemused best man from extreme embarrassment when he corrected a competitor's unfortunate spelling mistake on the bridesmaid's engraved gifts.

'How much do I owe?' asked the best man.
'Nothing,' replied Ashley.
'But it was my mistake,'
'Don't worry,' said Ashley, 'call it a wedding present.'

Adrian in Beverley, whose customer arrived at 4.55 p.m. with shoes that needed a full repair, is another of my heroes.

'Give me 20 minutes,' said Adrian.
'Sorry,' said the customer, 'my bus leaves at 5.16.'
'Not a problem,' said Adrian, 'I close at 5.00 anyway, so I'll get your shoes done straight away and give you a lift home.'

These are just two of the hundreds of good service stories that prove that Upside Down Management is working – compliments that come from customers who have benefited from our colleague's freedom to respond to a special situation. If we keep providing such exceptional customer care we will never need to advertise.

Looking back I must have been terribly naive. I thought that introducing my Upside Down Management style would be easy – but it wasn't. I made a lot of mistakes. I set out simply to improve our customer care but I didn't realise that in the process I was changing the whole business. I expected people in our shops to welcome the freedom I was giving them with open arms, but some didn't want it and others didn't trust me. I completely missed the point about personality. Upside Down Management doesn't suit everyone. Those who like to stick to rules and lazy people who expect to get money for nothing are untouched by it. Most of all, I totally underestimated the role of middle management – particularly our area managers. I soon discovered that Upside Down Management simply would not work unless the majority of our area managers gave it their vote.

We promote from within, so that everyone in our area teams – mobile managers, assistant area managers, area managers, regional managers and the field boss, Perry Watkins – started as apprentices. Their combined experience is invaluable; our 25 area and regional managers have together completed 600 years with Timpson. It was only when I spent a day out with one of the most experienced that I understood why they seemed to be so uncooperative. We had just visited a branch where two out of the three people should, in my view, have been classified as drongos and be destined to work for someone else, and I was impressing on the area manager the importance of having the right personalities.

Then he revealed the real problem. 'Apart from anything else,' he said, 'if I let my assistants do my job, what will be left for me to do?' That comment made me realise my mistake. I had changed the job of an area manager but I hadn't described what their new job was or how to do it.

I wrote an *Area Manager's Guide* that explained the new role in words and pictures. For the first time I really thought about what an area manager is there to do. The guide described their role as leaders who set an example, and it showed how they can help their team to run the area on their behalf. It demonstrated how to be a delegator and communicator and illustrated the importance of building a team, dealing with people problems and being an agony aunt. It completely redefined their job.

Writing that manual taught me how Upside Down Management applied to area managers who, unlike colleagues working in our shops, had to look in two directions. While giving branch colleagues the freedom to serve the customers in the way they thought best, each area manager had the freedom to run his area using initiative to achieve the best results. It took three months to write the manual, and when I had finished I realised that Upside Down Management was a culture that could affect every part of our company. I produced 250 pages of words and pictures covering every aspect of an area manager's job, but didn't send it out. At each Area Managers' Conference (three times a year) I revealed a little bit more of the area manager's role and gave them plenty of time to discuss the detail. Gradually the message started to sink in. One by one area managers changed their routine, delegating day-to-day management to their assistants and used the extra time to think about change and recruit the right people. Their success set an example. Upside Down Management had started to become part of the Timpson culture.

After that, it was time to tackle the biggest threat to Upside Down Management – Head Office. Most people think Head Office is there to tell everyone else what to do. People proudly talk about being promoted to Head Office where they can set policy and issue memos that they expect people in the field to read diligently and obey. Things have become worse since we've had computers, which give even more power to Head Office. Indeed, Head Office domination has been going on so long that branches assume that anything that comes from anyone based in Head Office is an order. Years ago, when I found something strange occurring in a branch, the answer was almost certainly going to be 'Someone from Head Office told me I had to.'

It's taken a few years but we've changed the culture. First, we stopped Head Office issuing any orders and told the branches to ignore any orders that slipped through. Secondly, we stopped everyone calling it Head Office – for the last few years it's been Timpson House. Then we set about explaining to people in the office that their job is to help our branch colleagues to run the business better – they're a support centre, not a dictatorship.

I didn't realise how much the office was getting in the way of our branches doing better business. Department heads were using area managers as messenger boys, expecting them to go from shop to shop to check on our stock of laces or to complete a report on which shops had a sanitary towel bin. The branches were run ragged by the number of requests and instructions. It was death by memo. We banned all memos, and everything now goes into our weekly news-letter. If someone from Timpson House rings a busy shop, he or she may have to be patient and wait, or may even receive the blunt response: 'We're full of customers, ring back later.'

It's important that people in the office understand what it's like to be in a shop. To get everyone out of the office, our annual Timpson House bonus is increased by 10% for anyone who spends a full day in a shop during the year. We're getting there. Our regular feedback from branch staff rating the departments at Timpson House is showing higher approval ratings each year. Yet we still have to remind some people not to walk past a ringing telephone, as it might be a branch that needs vital help. And, from time to time, I still catch someone issuing an order. Upside Down Management can never be taken for granted.

Our culture is unpopular with people whose priority is to pursue their own personal ambition. Politics, if allowed to flourish, can consume a lot of office energy. It has been said that 30% of executive time is spent pursuing individual rather than company goals. There is a notice in our lobby:

> **Leave your politics in the car park.**

I am always conscious of a strong magnetic force trying to bring us back in line with the world of command and control, because that's what other businesses do. Being a boss in an Upside Down Management world is an unselfish role that is a million miles away from the high-back chairs, flashy boardrooms and barked commands of *The Apprentice*. This is not an aggressive hire and fire business, it is a family where people work together like friends and help the people who serve the customers to run the business.

It is now 10 years since we decided to introduce Upside Down Management, and it is making a massive difference. Nevertheless, it is not easy to change a culture. Anyone who is thinking of following in our footsteps should take note of the vital ingredient that is needed to make it work: the Chief Executive must be the champion of Upside Down Management. He or she is the only person who can make it work. If you're in personnel, sales or marketing, don't dream of trying to introduce Upside Down Management until you have your CEO's 100% commitment. Upside Down Management is all-or-nothing, only the CEO can do this, and in doing so he or she must clearly understand how it will change everyone's job. The CEO must have the determination to replace orders, memos, KPIs and nitpicking with praise, lots of listening, and clear obstacles out of the way to give people true freedom to operate. The Chief Executive must be on a mission to change everyone's perception of management. Doing things upside down is nothing like what they teach at management school. In doing so, they must understand the importance of personality and identify the drongos who would obstruct progress.

Don't expect Upside Down Management to take root overnight. Give it plenty of time – you've got to promote it, sell it and nurture it. Everything has to be introduced by persuasion because that's the way you run an Upside Down business.

Upside Down Management may take years to establish, but eventually it *will* start to work. In an upside down company, everyone else starts to run the business, and your life in the boardroom becomes far less stressful as you sit back and watch your team produce better and better results. In case you're worried, however, there is still plenty left for the CEO to do – but more of that later.

Top tips

Here are my top tips for any brave company who would like Upside Down Management to work for them:

1. **The CEO must be 100% Committed.** Without the CEO's leadership, Upside Down Management simply will not work.
2. **Pick Personalities.** You need the right characters to make it work – positive people who like a challenge, not dull individuals who prefer convention and working to rules.
3. **No Compromise.** Upside Down Management can't be timid – you have to do everything wholeheartedly: trust everyone, give total freedom, and don't issue any orders.
4. **Be Patient.** It could take five years to establish an Upside Down Management culture.

Chapter Three

BE THE CEO

Under Upside Down Management, the Chief Executive can be just as upside down as everybody else. You have freedom to do the job in the way you think best, as long as you, in turn, give freedom to your team. If shareholders, the government or anyone else prescribes a process, ignore them – do it your way. All I offer are guidelines. These are my observations from 35 years of trying to do the job, but feel free to do what you want. All entrepreneurs create their success by being themselves.

Running a business is not the glamorous job that you read about in the financial press or see in the movies. Very little time is spent doing big deals and you certainly shouldn't sit behind a desk issuing orders and making snap decisions. Most of all don't spend your life in meetings. There are no rules. Business schools don't tell you how to be a Chief Executive. They provide the theory but not the practice. Read as many management books as you like, but 90% of your lessons will come from experience. Below is what my experience has taught me.

Real life leadership lessons

Trust your people

You can't run a business on your own, you need good people. Your job is to lead them by setting the style. Your people want to know who they are working for, and be guided by your expectations. Every business reflects the personality of its Chief Executive; think of Body Shop, Virgin or the changes that come with each Chief Executive at Marks & Spencer.

Give your people plenty of freedom and let them make their own decisions, but you must make the big decisions yourself. It's your job to define the main problems and find solutions that work. Don't spend time searching for the perfect answer – there are many possible strategies, choose one and stick to it. Don't delegate the job to a corporate planner, do it yourself. You must choose the overall direction and decide when change should happen.

Outsiders find it difficult to understand how, despite catching colleagues stealing money almost every week of the year, we are still able to trust people to handle the cash and even set their own prices. Suspicion is expensive, and every attempt to tighten security costs money. I have found it much cheaper to trust everybody, but watch them carefully as I've had many big disappointments: for example, people who have been working for the business for 30 years have been caught taking cash. I've had area managers who have abused their position by forcing shop colleagues to hand over money as they travel round the shops. But I still refuse to design a system around the 2% who are dishonest, I'd much rather give everyone else freedom so that the 98% of honest people are encouraged to make me more money.

Communicate

It's your job to communicate. It's no good having great ideas that don't become reality. Tell everyone the direction you want to take, and persuade them that it's the right way to go. Make things simple. We live in a complicated world full of information and regulations that interfere with doing good business. You are the only person who can clear the obstacles that obstruct your company's progress. You are the one who decides which management conventions the business should use and which should be ignored.

Pick a team who 'get it'

Everyone else in your company is probably better at their job than you are. If our success depended on my ability to cut keys we would have failed years ago. Thankfully key cutting is not my role. My job is to pick the right personalities and help them to create success.

I want to develop the people who 'get it'; people who understand the organisation and the way we want to run it. That implies lots of internal appointments. It's quicker that way because I don't have to explain Upside Down Management to a bewildered outsider. As the business gets bigger, more graduates appear, but degrees are not the main qualification – we still look for personality and the ability to make things happen. Personality is vital and it's your personality that will determine the overall success, so don't hide it, be yourself, show your passion, and don't run the business by following a set of rules. Follow your instinct.

Be a maverick

Don't be dominated by administrators, do it your way. Pen-pushers concentrate on saving money and writing rules that keep power concentrated at Head Office. Don't rely solely on your Finance Department for information. Get to know your organisation by relentlessly going round to meet your colleagues. And if you appear a little bit eccentric, so much the better. Face-to-face chats with people from every part of your business will tell you things you can't read in the management accounts. Accounts tell you about the past; your job is to decide the future. Your colleagues' comments and ideas carry more force than any consultant. There is one simple principle that makes the CEO's job much easier – the better he knows the business, the easier the business is to run.

Create a simple plan

Delegate all the day-to-day tasks but don't delegate strategy. Talk to lots of people before you make any big decisions.

but once you've made your decision don't invite further debate.

Upside Down Management gives the CEO more time to think. When you have the space to stand back and worry about the future the answer is often staring you in the face. Most successful business plans are based on a heavy dose of common sense, and often come with an inspirational flash of the obvious. You don't need genius, just a clear mind and some empty spaces in your diary.

You watch day-to-day problems at a distance but major capital decisions are down to you. Don't delegate the future of the company. You sign off the major capital projects and sit around the table when the big deals are done. Only make big decisions if the answer is obvious. If you don't know what to do, do nothing – sit on the fence and wait. When you know you have the right answer it is much easier to persuade everyone to follow your lead.

There is no need to write a thesis – no one needs to see your detailed analysis. Your colleagues just want to know your big ideas, why they will work, and why they will be of benefit to them.

Complicated plans lack clear thinking and very seldom work. Whoever first suggested that any report worth reading should be on one side of A4 got it exactly right. I would go further – write it in pictures with very few words.

Common sense

Your people will be grateful for their freedom; they don't want you to interfere, but they do want to see you and hear what you have to say. Communicate everything, not just the big decisions. Every time you talk to a colleague you strengthen his or her view of the company, that's why relentlessly going round the business is a wonderful way to run a company. It's not complicated, it's common sense. Most things are obvious.

People doing the day-to-day business know more about the company than you do. Take their advice. If they have a good idea let them try it. Concentrate on the important things, don't let politics and petty rules get in the way, and stick to the obvious decisions – the 'no brainers' – but a word of warning: don't rely on the figures, the only way to be certain what is happening is to check for yourself. That's common sense.

Have gaps in the diary

Some executives are impossible to tie down; they are so busy and so important that there's no space left in their diary to arrange an appointment for months ahead. Most of our deals are opportunistic, and to take advantage you need to act immediately. Most of these full diaries are caused by a strict timetable governed by lots of routine meetings. It is much better to vary your programme and occasionally do things differently, ensure that you keep your mind open to new ideas, and always leave some spare time to think.

When I was running the shoe shops, I was one of those busy executives who didn't have enough time. It was only when the shoe shops had been sold and I concentrated on shoe repairs that I changed my lifestyle. The shorter my working week, the better the business seemed to do; a workaholic Chief Executive doesn't necessarily make a business more profitable.

Know the business

The better you know the business the easier your job becomes. Every few weeks we have a residential course at Manchester when 30 to 35 new recruits come from around the country to spend two days becoming better acquainted with the business. Either James or I, or sometimes both of us, drop in on the course and rather than give a talk we go round the room asking the apprentices to state their name and where they work. We tell each one something about their shop, what it looks like, its history, a little about the managers, the shops next door, and any quirky fact that comes to mind. They are amazed at our knowledge but it's not difficult to remember, and we don't need briefing notes. James and I know every shop, because we've been there.

We remember the detail because we are interested, and knowing the business so well makes a big difference as it helps us to make quick decisions.

Meet as many people as you can

Every time you meet a colleague the business benefits. You learn more about what's going on and develop a feeling of mutual respect and trust. When a company gets into difficulty, management naturally becomes more introverted and there is an inclination to hold lots of internal meetings in a desperate attempt to find a solution. It is much better to cancel the meetings and go round the business.

The early 1990s were difficult. Sales fell dramatically and during the summer months we began to make a loss. If we had simply looked at the figures we would have started slashing costs, but we didn't, because when I went round the shops I realised that, despite the disappointing sales, we were doing better than the opposition. We were suffering because demand was down not because there was anything wrong with what we were doing. You can't make money in a market that has collapsed. We were patient. Some of our competitors fell by the wayside and eventually we bought Automagic, at almost the precise point when the market started to recover.

Keep going round the business

Occasionally a desk-bound Chief Executive sees the light and goes on a tour of his business, but after a few weeks or months he returns to his former lifestyle, and having ticked the travelling box his life can go back to normal. These people miss the point. Good Chief Executives don't regard travelling as an occasional chore, and it's not just part of their job; for them it is the way they do their job. I now spend at least two days a week going round our shops and James, very often, spends four. With the help of mobile phones and BlackBerrys it's just as easy to run the business while you are on the move. Indeed, you are less likely to be interrupted while you are driving down the M1.

We meet our people and hear the gossip. I don't need to watch *Coronation Street*, I have my own drama unfolding day by day. By visiting our shops every week I keep up with the plot.

Always pick up the phone

If the phone rings I pick it up; you never know who it may be. Admittedly I have to deal with some very irritating salesmen, some of whom become quite aggressive when I suggest that they will not be able to improve my bottom line. I don't want corporate tickets to Twickenham, nor do I need help with my personal investments. The irritating salesman has become a bit of a challenge. How quickly can I get them off the phone without being impolite?

As most Chief Executives have a PA to screen their calls, people are surprised when they get straight through to the Chief Executive, but you can use that element of surprise to your advantage. It helps when the call comes from a complaining customer. Customers are amazed when they are able to speak to the Chief Executive. It is even better if, having received a letter, you pick up the phone and ring the person who made the complaint. In my experience that nearly always turns the complaint into a compliment.

Only look at the information that matters
The trouble with this information age is that there is too much information. Your computer can give you millions of facts about your business, but you only need a few. I don't have a computer or a laptop in my office, which is probably a good thing; if I started surfing our data, I'd get distracted. I just need to see our cash position every day, the sales figures every week and the management accounts every month – I learn the rest by visiting our shops.

Interfere with training
Don't let your training department run the business. The training team constantly meets colleagues face to face. They are the ultimate day-to-day communicators, but you, as Chief Executive, must be head of communication. Your training

manager could, by default, write company policy. Training must be encouraged, but interfere as much as you can to ensure that the right message is being spread throughout the business. Do some training yourself. Every year James and I give a number of talks to outside conferences, but two years ago we decided to devote more of our talking to our own business. We now contribute to many training courses and run our own Leadership Course – a 24-hour midday-to-midday session for about 25 people, designed to explain our business philosophy and the way Upside Down Management works. There are plenty of syndicate sessions on the course, so we are not talking all the time, but whenever we receive feedback from delegates the one remark that stands out is: it makes a big difference that the course is run by John and James.

With our style of management we rely on our people to run the business, but it's our job to create the culture. Today, if you talk to Timpson people about Upside Down Management, I'm quite sure they'll know what you're talking about.

Barge into meetings

I am allergic to meetings, but I realise that some are necessary. The big time wasters are informal groups that turn themselves into standing committees, discussing the same points over and over again at regular intervals without reaching a major conclusion. As we don't tell people how to do their job, meetings are not forbidden, but I reserve the right to barge into any meeting and join the debate. It's another way of finding out what's going on and sometimes you find some surprises. One day Tina, who runs our Locksmith business, was talking to people from Victim Support. I joined in a quick conversation which led to a significant contract for home security surveys. That was a positive. I'm sure my colleagues would prefer that I didn't interfere, but I won't stop interrupting their meetings. All the meeting rooms in our new office have glass fronts, so everyone can see the meeting in progress, and it is now even easier for me to interrupt.

Muck in

Even though you are probably not good at doing many of the jobs that your colleagues do, have a go. Even if you can't cut a key, talk to customers when you are in a shop. You may learn something and you'll certainly be respected by your colleagues. Don't worry if you make a fool of yourself, as long as you apologise to the customer. One of the best ways to gain respect is to admit a mistake – apologising is a powerful way to enhance your reputation.

Spring lots of surprises

Don't be predictable. Change your routine regularly and find ways to give your best colleagues pleasant surprises. In September 2009 I was in Stratton Street, London, when Roberto, a branch colleague I know well, opened his briefcase. Inside were all the tools he needed to make a pair of shoes by hand. He'd made the thread, got the soling leather and the heel blocks; the only thing missing was a quality pair of uppers before he could start on his new hobby. Coincidently, the following day when I was sending letters to colleagues who have significant anniversaries at Timpson, I saw Roberto on the list. He'd been with Timpson for 10 years. As well as putting congratulations at the bottom of his letter I told him that we'd find the brand new pair of uppers he needed. Springing pleasant surprises is one of the best parts of running a business.

Random celebrations

We have lots of parties, award ceremonies and anniversary celebrations, but none of them is an annual event. The first time I had an office barbecue at our home it was a great success, so we had one the following year and more people came because they had found out how good the first one was. But when we did the third one, it just didn't have quite the buzz. I got the message, and we no longer have events that occur year after year. Every occasion now comes with an element of surprise.

Do what you are good at

Under Upside Down Management you should let your team get on with it, but if you want to get involved in the detail, stick to the bits you are good at. Don't be tempted to try everything as it will only make you look silly. Today your job is to be the Chief Executive. You need to be good at strategy and communication, it's fine to display your old skills occasionally, but you shouldn't get in the way, wait until you are asked. I know when I'm wanted when James says, 'Could you write something for the Newsletter?' or 'Did we face the same problem 30 years ago?'

Be the head of PR and communications

As Chief Executive you represent the company. Corporate communications cannot be delegated, people want to hear from you and only you can give the company's opinion. When the media ask for a company spokesman, that's you. You are the editor in chief of the company newsletter and write the company annual report.

At the end of 2007 we decided to stop spending on public relations. That didn't mean that we stopped talking to the press, we just issued no press releases and ceased chasing up the media. Since then we have had more publicity than ever before. We had a stroke of luck when James's younger brother Edward became the Conservative MP for Crewe and Nantwich at a high-profile by-election. Edward appeared on page three of *The Sun* with our Nantwich shop in the background. Then the media singled out shoe repairs as a likely beneficiary from the recession. Gradually more media activity came our way. Out of the blue *The Daily Telegraph* asked me to write a weekly agony column based on business, and several national newspapers and magazines did personal profiles. The most significant exposure came with a half-hour

Radio 4 programme made by Peter Day's *In Business*, which focused on Upside Down Management. Probably the main reason for all this free publicity is that James and I do it ourselves.

Resist consultants but have a guru

There is a big difference between consultants and gurus. I have always been fortunate to have someone at the end of the phone, so I can always discuss problems with someone I can trust. I consult Roger and Patrick, my two non-executive directors, and Michael McAvoy who has advised me on corporate communications since 1975. They know me and our business well enough to tell me when I've got it wrong. That advice is very different from consultancy. Consultants are fine as long as they're doing a job that no one in the business can do, but using consultants to do your forward planning is a cop out – strategy is your job, that's what the Chief Executive does. Use consultants sparingly (if at all); they are a desperate measure to help you out when you don't know where to turn. If you get to the stage where you need consultants to adjust your strategy, they may advise that you, the CEO, should be replaced by someone else.

Get involved in marketing

The marketing function has too much influence on the future of the business to have the full freedom of Upside Down Management. We don't have a marketing department; James and I do that job. Most other companies would consider the abandonment of marketing to be unthinkable, but as Chief Executive I would always want to know what the marketing people are doing as they have too much influence to be left to their own devices.

Write your own business plan

Some big companies have a corporate planning and strategy department – I do it myself. I wouldn't delegate the role to anyone else as the Chief Executive should chart the future of the company.

Send hand-written notes

E-mails have put a premium on the hand-written letter. The way to praise people or to let them know that you really care is to write a personal letter. Use a fountain pen, write the envelope yourself, send it to their home address and put on a proper stamp. That is the most powerful way you can communicate to every colleague from Board Director to Sales Assistant.

Promote personalities

I believe in promoting internal candidates to our top jobs. We take succession planning very seriously and there is a strong chance that nearly every future vacancy will be filled by a home-grown candidate. I haven't advertised for a senior executive for over five years, but if I did I'd avoid a lot of the gobbledegook that you see on the appointment pages.

One said:

The successful candidate is someone who can create a world-class operation through superior management methodology. The brief calls for proactive leadership in standard setting and monitoring, underpinned by effective resource optimisation. The challenge is to grasp the nettle and instil or install an ethos of measurement, accountability and delivery. You must have proven substantive experience gained at a rigorous leading edge environment, underpinned with a track record of business improvement and cultural change using analysis, KPIs and strident review.

Another was looking for candidates who were:

... familiar with leading edge planning and forecasting tools and could drive through best practice by taking the lead in cross-functional meetings.

And, a third wanted people who could:

... provide evidence of demonstrable success in developing benchmark processed and competency models having gained experience in devising and managing learning and development solutions.

Avoiding the jargon I would look for someone with the right personality and values. Someone who's down to earth and, whatever the size of enterprise, is still able to act as if it was a small business and can do the job without the help of a big empire and an army of advisers. I want someone who is cost conscious, having the nose for spotting useless expenditure and unnecessary jobs. My ideal candidate must aim to be the best in all that he or she does; mediocrity is not good enough – 'it'll do' will *not* do.

In the quest for success the candidate will love change and always want to get better. I want someone who has the courage to banish bureaucracy and buys into the idea of Upside Down Management. I'm looking for somebody who will take a chance, but admit his or her mistakes. Most of all, I'd be looking for a personality who enjoys the job, is admired by his or her colleagues and brings fun to the workplace.

Here is my advert:

Timpson seeks a paranoid personality who relies on common sense. A permanent pessimist with an open mind, a perennial optimist who can admit mistakes, a dedicated delegator with the courage to take big decisions. A mean eye for cost control but generous at handing out praise; a stickler for standards but loves new ideas, knows how to celebrate success, but always aims to do better. In short – I want someone who has 'got it'. Big shots and empire builders need not apply.

Signs of a second-rate CEO

These are the things that I think can make a CEO great. But over the years I have seen the tell-tale signs that a CEO has not 'got it'. Even some of the most inspirational Chief Executives exhibit some of the traits I list below. If you find somebody who demonstrates three, or even more, of these second-rate boss signals, it is time to worry.

Back-to-back meetings

Someone who spends his life in meetings isn't delegating, doesn't get round the business and hasn't got the time in his diary to plan for the future.

We had problem with a business that was helping us to develop a website. Things got so bad that James decided to intervene and give the Managing Director a final chance before we closed the contract. He rang to discuss the problem, but got through to his PA. 'He's not available,' she said. James explained the problem and the reason he wanted to speak to him urgently.

> 'He's in back-to-back meetings all day,' she said. 'I suggest you leave a message.'
>
> 'I've just told you what I wanted to talk about,' said James.
>
> 'Send an e-mail,' said the PA.
>
> 'I don't do e-mails,' said James. 'I prefer to talk to people in person.'

'You can,' she said, 'as long as you send an e-mail first.'

'But I've given you my message,' said James.

'No, if you won't send an e-mail he won't talk to you, that's our system; he has a busy schedule.'

James never did talk to him. We simply terminated the contract.

Gobbledegook

I don't know what's wrong with simple English. Some executives seem to spend their lives inventing words and phrases that I can't understand. Some send spam e-mails to my BlackBerry. Here is one of the worst offenders:

> *We are a leading global provider of business process optimisation and outsourcing solutions. Our business changing delivery is achieved by removing the information overload and providing intuitive, searchable information architecture which delivers project visibility and control through integrated multi-user project services. Please let me know when it is convenient to talk to you.*

The answer is never. People who use gobbledegook find it difficult to understand the simple words – common sense.

Spin doctors

The recent recession has been a bonanza for spin doctors – people who lie in the company's interest. A business I know has been having a bad run, but their share price recovered following an interim statement, because they claimed the trading out-turn was 'well beyond their expectations'. In truth, sales were 7.5% down and profits had halved.

The real guilty parties here are the analysts who are taken in by the trickery, but beware of executives who rely on the use of spin. I would much rather back people who consistently tell the truth and get on with running the business.

Stubbornness

I have seen several instances of Chief Executives who stubbornly stick to their chosen policy while everyone around them tells them it is going wrong. This is a sign of someone who runs things from Head Office, believing that his job is to make sure that everyone else agrees with policy. Automagic was a good example. The Managing Director, and main shareholder, didn't see the need to change. His original shoe repair business had been extremely successful and he resented the need to introduce key cutting. It was a stubborn act that, in the end, cost him the business. People who stick with their pet project through thick and thin think they are showing leadership, but in truth they demonstrate insensitive ignorance.

Faith in foolish people

In nearly every acquisition we have discovered executives in senior positions who block progress. These people have no respect for the rest of the workforce and make a major contribution to the company's failure. The existence of senior executive drongos demonstrates a major flaw in the Chief Executive, who should have sorted out the problem by saying goodbye to the executives many years before. While we were negotiating one of our major acquisitions, we were well aware that the senior field manager was a real problem. When we finally bought the business and started talking to branch colleagues, they only had two questions:

1. Are you going to close my shop?
2. What's happened to the Sales Director?

When I told them that he left the day we bought the business they were delighted and began to realise that we knew how to run their business.

Drongos picking drongos

One drongo executive can do harm enough, but things get worse when they start recruiting people like themselves. They are often poor managers and very good politicians. If the drongo group gets too big, the whole business can collapse.

If you think one drongo executive is bad enough, let me introduce you to two dangerous and stress-making individuals. They will claim that they are doing an excellent job on behalf of the business, but they actually get in the way of progress. First there is Mr Ahbut. He prides himself on being the devil's advocate, the permanent in-house risk assessor, ready to tell you all the reasons why something won't work. He enjoys analysing problems, writing reports and sitting through endless meetings without ever reaching a conclusion. Mr Ahbut is probably not as dangerous as his friend, Mr Gunna. He agrees with everything and is everyone's friend, fully supporting company policy. Mr Gunna is always about to do it, but is full of excuses why the job has not been done.

'It's the next thing on my list,' he says.

'I'm glad you raised that, I'll give it a higher priority.'

'I can't do it now until we've finished the budget.'

'It would have been done a long time ago, but we're short staffed.'

'I've got it scheduled in my next list of things to do.'

With Mr Ahbut telling you why things can't be done, and Mr Gunna avoiding things he knows he needs to do, your life becomes a misery. The only solution is to get rid of them both and replace them with Mr Got It.

The empire builder

Beware the new executive whose first concern is the size of his office and the make of his car. You can almost guarantee that within weeks he will be recruiting colleagues from his past job, including his previous PA. If you don't watch things carefully, before you know it you'll find that a small empire has been built with a life of its own, costs go up and a new political party has been born within your business. David Edwards, who joined us to help to run the Max Spielmann business, didn't have an office or a PA. He didn't run his own empire, he simply helped us to run the business.

The consultant's friend

Too many businessmen bring in consultants and market researchers to do their job. It is the Chief Executive's role to make decisions: there are plenty of people to consult who already work for the business. It is rarely necessary to bring in outsiders, but for many executives it's the first thing they do. Some of the biggest mistakes are the result of market research, with statistical boffins using a survey of, sometimes, no more than 500 people which is used to determine future strategy.

The market researchers and consultants could not have got it more wrong for Mr Minit when they produced their format for Minit Solutions. Their multi-service concept was a very good idea and will probably become an important part of Timpson, but Minit decided that shoe repairs should be hidden out of sight. 'Clean and dirty don't mix,' said the market researchers – which was a catchy phrase that caught the imagination of Minit management. As a result they hid their shoe repairs from view and sales fell by 50%.

I had seen the days in the 1960s when shoe repairs were brought out of the back shop and put in front of the public, bringing an instant 60% increase in turnover, so I wasn't surprised when the new Minit shops failed to perform. Market research is no substitute for experience.

Short-term cost cutting

Some Chief Executives, particularly those who flit from one company to another every three years, like to make money by cutting costs. This strategy can produce short-term improvements, but is not the basis for long-term success. Every business goes through a few difficult times. On each occasion the Finance Director is likely to step forward and propose a cost-cutting campaign.

I met my first crisis in 1975; my Finance Director offered to chair a cost-cutting committee and stupidly I agreed. For a month his committee took control and played business politics. 'In my hardworking department, costs are already cut to the bone,' each department head pleaded. The operations director was not there, he was busy running his shops, so the committee proposed cuts out in the field. 'Shop wages are our biggest cost; to make an impact we must cut the staff who serve our customers,' they argued. Thankfully I rejected their plans and left the committee to concentrate on some hair-shirt economies, Spartan measures for difficult times. They cut out Christmas parties, free fruit and the *Financial Times* in reception, which no one read. They even counted the loo paper: we used a roll per person per fortnight. This attention to detail pleased our Finance Director: 'It's creating the right atmosphere,' he said as he launched his 'save-it' campaign by putting red stickers by every light switch.

These irritating small economies don't do lasting damage, but I saw another Finance Director (thankfully not mine) champion a cost-cutting campaign that ruined his business. During difficult times Finance Directors often make decisions which they claim are essential. Sales had dropped 12% and were getting worse, but this Finance Director knew nothing about retailing. 'To meet budgeted profits, wages must be brought in line with turnover,' he said, 'and margins must be increased to make up the shortfall.' He got his way. Prices went up, staffing went down, and sales plummeted a further 10%. The Finance Director, still keen to make up the profit shortfall, ordered more price increases and redundancies, which put the company into administration. Cost cutting is fine as long as you are cutting out costs you don't need and have a vision for the future.

Puffed up

Years ago some of our shop managers changed character overnight when they were promoted to the role of area manager. They bought themselves a suit and a briefcase and immediately thought they were superior to the rest of their team. Chief Executives can do the same thing, treating their office as an ivory tower in the belief that they are now a cut above everyone else in the business. They quickly lose touch with reality, because although they talk to colleagues, it's always at a meeting or a big style conference; they never tour the business to meet people face to face.

I remember when I was a shop assistant in my first job, a senior director came to call. He never spoke to me; I might as well not have been there, and I have never forgotten it. Every time I visit one of our shops I try to make sure that I talk to everyone.

Top-down communications

On a few occasions during my career I have experienced a formalised communication system where, every quarter, information is cascaded down from the top through a series of meetings until the corporate message eventually arrives at the shop floor. Despite carefully prepared briefing notes, the message quickly gets tired as it travels through the organisation.

Our weekly newsletter works well, but the best form of communication is face to face. People like to hear from the Chief Executive, and that's why James holds his Town Hall meetings when he talks to everyone in the office each month. As soon as you rely on someone else to spread the word, something gets lost in translation.

Mission statements

It is dangerous to think that a mission statement thought up by committee can clarify a company's objectives and communicate the strategy throughout the business. People who rely on mission statements often like gobbledygook (see earlier), and most mission statements simply state the obvious. Everyone wants to be best in class while providing an amazing customer experience, but these statements don't work unless you've got the right people – and if you've got the right people, you don't need a mission statement. Smart phrases seldom create success; the priority is to have a team of people who 'get it'.

* * * * *

Any boss who displays several of the attributes that I have just described above would find it impossible to practise Upside Down Management. Control freaks don't let go enough to delegate. They don't trust their team to deal with the detail, so they run the business by issuing orders and constantly interfering.

These people never have time to step up to the real job of a Chief Executive; they don't realise that when you are released from issuing orders, sending memos, doing the budget and carrying out appraisals, there is still plenty to do. Indeed, you have created the precious time you need to do the real job of a CEO.

- Don't spend every day behind a desk. If you have too much paperwork, pick out anything important and put the rest in the bin.
- Don't put on an act, be yourself, display your emotions, share your joys and disappointments and, most of all, be visible.

You can't run a business if the business doesn't know who you are. If you're the conductor of the orchestra, you don't play any instrument but the players expect you to set the tempo and create the excitement.

CEOs who 'get it'

Despite the hard work of business schools, writers of business books and the development of management science, the best companies are still run by personalities who rely on flair and experience. This is further proof that management is an art, not a science. Fortunately each generation produces a number of instinctive entrepreneurs who are able to perform miracles.

Here are a few of the entrepreneurs and business leaders who have inspired me:

- *Harry Levison*, who developed the British Shoe Corporation, was a tough uncompromising genius. Having started running a shoe business in the east end of London he created a chain of over 2,000 shops using a combination of takeover bids, shrewd property dealing and good shoe buying.

- *Marcus Sieff* – It's becoming quite difficult to remember how dominant Marks & Spencer used to be on Britain's high street. Marcus Sieff set a standard for other retailers to follow by creating a company that offered great value and was the best place to work. It was a very disciplined approach, but still had plenty of room for new ideas.

- *John Speden-Lewis* created the John Lewis Partnership and made all his employees shareholders – an inspirational idea that has survived the test of time. Lots of companies have introduced profit-sharing schemes and given employees the opportunity to purchase equity, but no one has done more to change a business culture than John Speden-Lewis.

- *Ralph Halpern* who rescued the Burton Group and changed the face of Britain's high street in the 1980s; he had a colourful lifestyle which overshadowed his genius as a retailer. When he got involved, Burton was a basket case, a business based on made-to-measure suits. He completely transformed Burton by introducing fashion merchandise at value prices in a revolutionary new generation of shop design. Burton's real success was in the property market. Halpern used his collection of brands to juggle the property portfolio and spread all his businesses, Burton, Top Shop, Top Man, Principles and Dorothy Perkins, onto every major high street.

- *The Lewis Family*, originally owners of Chelsea Girl, performed one of the most stunning transformations the high street has ever seen. Chelsea Girl changed overnight to become River Island, a format that has continually been updated and kept in the forefront of one of the most competitive sectors of the high street.

- *Terence Conran* has been given credit for the introduction of lifestyle retailing in the UK, but his success is much more than that. He got involved in retailing because he was producing products that the retail trade would not put on sale. Conran has had influence on a number of high street names, not just Habitat, Mothercare and Richard Shops, Heals, and, more recently, his restaurant businesses, but Terence was also Chairman of Hepworths and together with fellow director, Trevor Morgan, bought Kendalls Rainwear, which was then turned into Next. Although George Davis (see below) is credited with the invention of Next it was, in fact, Terence Conran and Trevor Morgan who brought Next into the world.

- *George Davis* has to be given credit for inspiring Next one of the most influential retail names of the last 30 years. Despite the fact that an irresponsible period of expansion nearly killed the business, George Davis remains an inspirational retailer. He is a buyer and an innovator who thinks in terms of ranges that can be promoted in shops that become a theatre. His passion for new ideas has influenced all fashion retailing over 30 years.

- *Arnold Weinstock* developed GEC into a fabulous business by single-minded attention to detail and the confidence that only comes with a clear vision of the future. The importance of a sure hand and consistency was dramatically demonstrated by the decline of the business once Arnold Weinstock had retired.

- *Michael Bishop* had the determination to succeed from a very young age. Always interested in aircraft, he became the majority shareholder of British Midland Airways when he was only 30, following a management buyout. He developed a strong business in one of the most challenging industries. He continued to hold over 50% of the equity, while developing a major airline. He used his position to challenge authority in the name of common sense.

- *Richard Branson* perfectly demonstrates how a business can be dominated by the personality of its Chief Executive. He has shown the rest of us how to truly lead from the front.

- *Ken Morrison* – His reputation took a knock towards the end of his career when he bought Safeway, but, like most of the things he did, it was another correct decision. It took some time to integrate the two businesses, but now everyone's forgotten about Safeway and Morrison has become a national chain. The reputation of the business is restored and we can look back to Ken Morrison's career and see how his single-minded vision of the supermarket has created success.

- *Stanley Kalms* – Our most successful entrepreneurs are able to guide a business through several stages of development. Stanley Kalms took his family camera business and turned it into the first technology shop on the high street, achieving a dramatic takeover of Curry's and even at one time including the SupaSnaps business among its portfolio. This is another example of an entrepreneur leading a business that lost momentum when he retired.

- *Anita Roddick* turned an idea into an institution as a result of her personality and personal commitment. Ethical cosmetic retailing would not exist if it hadn't been for Anita Roddick. The Body Shop was one of the most dramatic retail developments of the last 50 years.

- *Liisa Joronen* is the driving force behind Sol, who employs over 3,000 office cleaners mainly in Finland. Her operation is the only other genuine upside down business I have ever seen. Everyone wears yellow and they are all empowered to do what they can to improve the business. She passionately defies convention and authority. To make the point, there are 100 wooden lemmings running along the skirting board of the living room at her home. All the lemmings are brown, except three who are painted yellow and run in the opposite direction.

All these people had the vision and personality to create a great business. The country needs characters like them with their personality and warrior spirit. We don't want plastic captains of industry who adhere to every directive, stick closely to government guidelines, get buried in budgets and risk assessments, delegate strategy to consultants, and are unwilling to take risks or to take the blame when their short-term cost-cutting measures fail to deliver long-term profits. We want people who get it, can do it their way, and have a vision for the future.

Both government and business are obsessed by process in the belief that management is a science. We need Chief Executives who will ignore governance and best practice but have the courage to run their business the way they know best – that is the freedom a Chief Executive gets with Upside Down Management.

Chapter Four

DO THE DEALS

Our shoe shops failed to go on the takeover trail. We watched British Shoe Corporation grab 25% of the market, and I eventually had to sell the business. Our shoe repair chain would not have survived without doing a series of deals. Acquisitions and disposals have created today's business.

Deals form a fundamental part of our strategy but there is so much that can go wrong. Every transaction teaches me new lessons about people, lawyers, accountants, bankers, ethics and people under pressure. I have also learned a lot about myself.

Despite the fact that every deal is so different, some items always seem to apply. You must be patient; lawyers and accountants work at a different pace – they are pedantic, they like detail. You might see the transaction as a straight-forward commercial deal but the game they play is fought clause by clause and you must be particularly patient in the early stages. I stalked BSC for 2 years, Automagic for 9 and

Mr Minit for 12. Deals don't appear just when you want them; you must cultivate them.

It helps to know more than your opposite number about the business you're buying. Don't just rely on the figures. Go and see the business, meet some of its people and understand its culture. If you are selling, it helps to have a naive buyer who takes figures at face value. Before negotiating be clear where to draw the line – if buying, set your top price; if selling, know the least you will accept. Think of the deal from the other side's point of view, work out what they are thinking and guess the price they are looking for.

Write the business plan yourself. Don't delegate the task to a merchant banker or your Finance Director. You are the person who must decide how to make the deal successful and what to say to your bank.

Deals are a big distraction, so you mustn't let your day-to-day business fall apart during negotiations. Expect surprises. I have only done one deal where the final agreement was identical to the 'heads of terms' (the original document that sets out the main points you have agreed with the other side before the lawyers get to work). Keep in touch with your opposite number. Lawyers bicker among themselves so much that they can make enemies out of the best of friends. If your lawyer thinks their lawyer is being unreasonable, short circuit the system and talk to the CEO on the other side.

When the deal is signed and the champagne drunk, you will wake up the following morning wondering what you could have done better. You may even think you have made a big mistake as deals nearly always come with a sizable hangover. Everything will usually prove worthwhile, but be careful as some transactions have led to disaster.

Don't assume that you can improve an acquisition overnight. It takes time to win the trust of your new colleagues. To improve cash flow and satisfy your bank manager, you should have lots of cost savings up your sleeve. The easiest way to save money is to close a head office.

Before starting any deal you must be able to answer these questions.

1. Does it fit in with your strategy?

As few countries have a chain like Timpson, we get regular requests to expand overseas. Despite the challenge, I'm not tempted. We know how to motivate the English, Scots and Welsh and are beginning to understand the Irish (where we have only been involved for six years). We keep in touch by relentlessly visiting shops to meet the people who meet the customers; we talk their language and they understand our culture, but I don't think we could do the same in France,

Germany, the USA or China. Expansion overseas is not for us. When we receive an approach, the answer is a firm 'No'.

2. Will the deal increase profits and improve your cash flow?

Why do a deal if it won't improve your business? You should only get involved where success seems a certainty.

3. What will happen in the first year?

Work out what you are going to do with the new business before you start negotiations. Have a picture in your mind of the first 12 months before you make an offer.

4. Who is going to run it?

Success in deals, as with so much else, will depend on people. Keep an open mind about the new colleagues you acquire. You will discover lots of talent but make sure your own Finance Director looks after the money and pick the CEO from your own business. The only way to get the culture right and establish your style of management is to put your own people in charge.

5. What are you doing it for?

People get a buzz from doing deals (for accountants and lawyers it is their cup final), but will it make your life easier and will you be better off? Every business needs to grow – bigger businesses are often easier to run – but are you sure it is worth the hassle?

6. What is the risk?

I was taught at university that profit is the reward for taking risks. That is misleading; risks should be avoided whenever possible. Look out for racing certainties, and never risk the existing business.

7. How is your current trade?

Acquisitions take more time than you think. Don't get involved without a good accountant, a good lawyer and lots of patience. Are you confident your management team can look after the shop while you are away having fun?

The stages of the deal

All the questions above need a positive answer before you press the button and start negotiating in earnest. Buying a business always takes longer than you imagine. It is an assault course with a predictable pattern; once terms are agreed and the paperwork gets under way, you will take a back seat while, on your behalf, others engage in nit-picking negotiations that often seem unnecessary. Here are the hoops through which you have to jump:

The courtship

You probably have a shortlist of possible acquisitions but it is unlikely that any are ready to be bought out. There is no point in being pushy, try to become their best friend and let them know that if they want to sell, you are a buyer. Then wait. You can't buy unless they want to sell, and you shouldn't buy unless the price is right. Polite patience is the order of the day but always keep in touch. A non-business example of this is the cottage in the foothills of Snowdon that my late mother-in-law lived in until 1988 when she sold it and moved to Cheshire. Alex and I saw it on a trip down memory lane 10 years later, but it was very run down. We knocked on the door but the occupant was out, so Alex left a note: 'This was my mother's house. If you ever want to sell, give me a ring; here is my home telephone number.' Seven years later the owner called and now the cottage is our latest Timpson holiday home.

Confidential information

Deals don't get started until you sign a confidentiality letter showing that the other side is willing to talk and provide the chance to obtain detailed information. Your Finance Director will ask his opposite number for volumes of figures, but the opposition will try to supply you with as little information as possible, and only give you the big numbers when you want detail. They will hide behind EBITDA (Earnings before Interest, Tax, Depreciation, and Amortisation) while you want to know the true profit and cash flow. During this phase of the deal, clear your desk and concentrate on the target. Dig so deep that you know the business better than anyone else in the world and don't let anyone (even your Finance Director) analyse figures on your behalf. Do it yourself, and continue to play with the numbers until you really understand them. Only you can decide whether the business is worth buying, and at what price. When you know enough, it is time to negotiate and agree heads of terms, but don't be deceived. You might have agreed a deal but it hasn't yet been done; there is still a long way to go. You have merely given a signal to lawyers to produce several draft agreements and start arguing with their opposite number.

Set a deadline

There is no limit to the legal points lawyers can raise. With meetings charged at an hourly rate, the longer the deal the larger the bill, but there is a limit. Lawyers realise that if they argue over petty clauses for too long their clients could disappear and they wouldn't collect a fee. Thankfully the hour finally comes (usually in the middle of the night) when you are given lots of papers to sign. When they have been stacked into a neat pile and your lawyer shakes your hand, the deal is complete.

At the outset, find an excuse to set the final date. It doesn't matter what the deadline is as long as it sounds credible – your year end, Christmas, the tax year or even your annual holiday are good reasons to get things done.

The morning after

The adrenalin has been flowing for months but you only recognise the pressure when it is all over, and you suddenly realise how much thinking time the deal has taken. Don't be surprised if you sleep for nearly 24 hours. When you wake up you will have a bigger business and never want to do another deal. But acquisitions are the way to grow and it won't be long before you are looking around for opportunities.

My deals

So that's how it works in theory, but, as I've said already, business is about practice not theory. To give you an idea of how it actually comes together here are some of the biggest, most stressful, challenging and interesting deals that I've done:

The buyout

Our management buyout threw me in at the deep end. Suddenly, instead of being a cog in a corporate wheel I had to take decisions on my own. Once Alex had persuaded me not to worry about the risk, I took the advice of my new-found lawyer friend Roger Lane-Smith, broke the confidentiality terms of my service contract, and started discussions with Candover, our venture capitalists. After an hour with Roger Brook at the Candover office I started to understand the mechanics of a buyout. He showed enough interest in Timpson to suggest a second meeting, but I needed to involve our Finance Director, Peter Cookson – another breach of confidentiality.

Timpson was making £2.5 million a year but the asset value was nearly £40 million. The key to doing a deal was to use the assets to fund the purchase. Timpson still held most of the freehold property purchased by my grandfather in the 1930s. I met Paul Orchard-Lyle from Healey & Baker who identified £30 million worth of property assets that could be sold on a sale and lease-back basis with an initial rental charge of £1.8 million. We were already being charged a market rent by UDS before producing our profit of £2.5 million. Based on Paul's figures, the rent charge would increase by £800,000, still leaving a profit of £1.7 million for Timpson. We could fund a substantial purchase price and still make money.

To make progress I had to speak to UDS who had never sold a business and were unlikely to change the habit of a lifetime. I was nervous about putting the proposition to Stuart Lyons. He had shown me considerable trust and I respected him for that. To suggest a buyout could be considered disloyal.

UDS was going through an even more torrid time than usual. As there were regular press stories about an imminent bid, this gave me the chance to talk to Stuart about the future of the group and Timpson's role within it. I said that if UDS had any thoughts of selling Timpson, they should consider me as a serious buyer. I followed up my meeting with this letter:

Dear Stuart
I was pleased to have your assurance that there is no truth in current rumours regarding Timpson and I hope

you appreciate the reasons for my concern. For the record I would like to reiterate that if there were a change and we became a candidate for asset realisation I should hope to be kept informed and despite the potential sum involved be given the opportunity to raise the finance necessary to purchase the Timpson business. I sincerely believe that my style of management is the best way to provide a good profit performance for Timpson shops and Timpson shoe repair, something I am sure we will provide in the second half of this year.
Yours John

I had made my first approach and no harm had been done, Stuart made it clear that Timpson had a firm part in the future strategy of UDS and there was no thought of selling our business. As far as I was concerned, the buyout plan had become an unrealised dream.

Everything changed in January 1983. I was visiting our shop in Hounslow when Patrick Farmer (MD of the Farmer shoe chain, another UDS subsidiary) rang to report a bid from a new group called Bassishaw. Backed by Heron, the Coal Board Pension Fund and Barclays Merchant Bank, the group was led by Gerald Ronson. They made an offer of 100 pence per share. I rang Roger Lane-Smith who was on holiday in the Cayman Islands and we decided to renew discussions with Candover as soon as he returned. During the next 10 days I flew to London five times for management meetings.

It was clear that UDS would never be the same again. The Lyons family had lost control and the business was being run by their merchant bank, Hill Samuel, whose takeover defence relied on selling John Collier and Richard Shops to the Burton Group and replacing the Lyons family with a new management team.

I decided to let Trevor Swete of Hill Samuel know about our plans. With Candover, we now estimated that the cash available from sale and lease-backs was around £32 million. Our annual profits of £2.2 million would be reduced to £1.4 million by the extra rent following the property sale. We decided we could pay at least £37.5 million and agreed to make a starting offer of £35 million.

Stephen Curran of Candover approached Trevor Swete who confirmed to me the following morning: 'Timpson is not for sale.' It soon became clear that Hill Samuel was close to selling Richard Shops and John Collier to the Burton Group (a deal is getting serious when the lawyers invent code names – Burton was Blue, Richards Red and John Collier White). We had a number of shoe concessions within John Collier and Richards, so I met the Burton Concessions Director, Tony Colman, to work out how our concessions would fit into their deal. But before Bassishaw or Hill Samuel got the chance to run UDS, Hanson Trust entered the ring with a knockout bid and won control of UDS.

Five months with Hanson was enough to tell me I could never be a corporate clone in a colossal company. The 20 people at their Brompton Road Head Office had all the fun. After three weeks Tony Alexander, who managed their UK business, asked me to visit him at Brompton Road. Candover agreed that I could use their name and suggested an offer of £36 million. Tony Alexander did not give an answer but he didn't say no. It was a first step.

Over the next few weeks I tried to persuade Hanson that Timpson was a business worth selling. We were trading on a very competitive high street, occupying shops with high rents in a sector reliant on the vagaries of fashion. The Hanson team paid several visits to Manchester, giving me ample opportunity to get my message across. Roger Lane-Smith had his own Hanson contact. He met Sir Gordon White, James Hanson's right-hand man, at a cocktail party in New York, and Roger considered that to be enough of an introduction to allow him to ring the USA and tell Sir Gordon about the Timpson buyout. Sir Gordon arranged to meet Roger on his next visit to London.

I was in Venice on a buying trip when the call came. Sir Gordon was over for Royal Ascot and agreed to see Roger and talk about Timpson. The meeting with Sir Gordon was cordial but inconclusive. We established that Timpson was for sale, but our offer of £35 million was inadequate – Hanson wanted £46 million. The problem was capital gains.

The book value of Timpson was £28.6 million (the price paid by UDS), and anything over that figure would attract tax at the rate of 33%. Sir Gordon White sent us away with a challenge: if we could cut their capital gains tax we might be close to a deal. Within days Peter Cookson had a solution. By separating the property transaction from the purchase of the company we established a capital loss on one deal that could be offset against the other. We solved Hanson's problem and also demonstrated our determination.

Conversations at Candover got more serious. We started to discuss the management of our new business and agreed that Trevor Morgan should be our prospective Chairman. Trevor was known to Candover Director, Michael Stoddart, and I had known Trevor for years. He was Chief Executive of Turners Footwear – I met him at meetings of the Multiple Shoe Retailers Association. He sold Turners to Hepworth who made him a main Board Director. Trevor introduced George Davis to Hepworth's and helped him set up Next.

While the Hanson Trust talked to us they also discussed deals involving other UDS companies. They progressed the deal that Hill Samuel had started with the Burton Group involving John Collier and Richard Shops but Ralph Halpern kept chipping at the price until Hanson became irritated. As a result, John Collier was sold to the management and Terence Conran's Storehouse bought Richard Shops.

Candover offered us their standard management share package. The Timpson team would subscribe £125,000 for 12½% of the equity, which could increase to 25% depending on performance. The other equity would be held by Candover and venture capitalists who were part of their club.

At our next meeting with Hanson I met Tony Alexander and his fellow director, Alan Hagdrup. Our latest figures suggested that we could safely offer £40 million with an absolute maximum of £42.5 million. I went to Brompton Road with Roger Lane-Smith and Stephen Curran of Candover, but the meeting didn't last long.

After confirming we had solved the tax problem Tony Alexander declared that he still wanted £44 million compared with our offer of £38 million.

It took less than an hour to agree the price that changed my life. We moved to £40 million. They moved to £42 million – a price that we agreed with the last £2 million to be paid over the next three years. The meeting started at 5.30 p.m. Within an hour whisky was poured to celebrate the deal. I thought, with terms agreed, it was all over bar the shouting. I did not realise that the deal had just begun. That night, I was so excited I couldn't sleep, but the following morning brought me back to reality. We needed £34 million from the sale and lease-back deals, but several phone calls from Paul Orchard Lyle suggested that this was by no means certain.

Back home I got a big shock. Peter Cookson rang: 'I have discovered a mistake.' My heart sank. 'We are £4 million better off,' he continued. 'I'll check the figures again tonight.'

The difference was due to intercompany balances; our original forecast had been based on completion in April, and it was now June. Our stockholding was much higher than budget and UDS had paid the bills on Timpson's behalf. When agreeing the deal Tony Alexander stopped any further intercompany transactions. This clarified our cash position and suddenly the whole deal was £4 million better than expected. Peter Cookson and his team worked the weekend to confirm the figures. By Sunday night it was clear that we were sitting in the pound seats.

I quickly saw the significance and seized the opportunity. On Sunday night I agreed with Roger that management should aim for 80% of the equity. The following morning David Briggs, the senior partner of our accountants, Peat Marwick, verified our figures. I saw Alan Jones, our manager at NatWest in Manchester, who confirmed their support. The deal was bankable, but we wanted to continue the Candover contact – we didn't want Hanson to think we'd a comfortable ride financing the deal. Roger Lane-Smith rang Stephen Curran at Candover to explain how the figures had changed and say that we were now looking for 80% instead of the 12½% on offer. Stephen offered 25%, then moved to 50% and finally conceded: 'I see where you're coming from.'

Our agreement with Hanson was just one of a number of deals to be negotiated. The list was a long one – property agents, property investors, venture capitalists, Candover, and the lawyers. Everyone wanted a lick of the spoon. Allocating the equity was my most difficult task. I tried to be fair but never forgot the problems my father suffered years earlier. I wanted control. I finished with 54%, and my four senior directors got 5% each. Roger took 2½% with the balance split between two subsidiary directors, my sister and our corporate communications adviser, Michael McAvoy.

Despite NatWest support we still planned to raise £2.5 million from the venture capitalists. After a fairly testing presentation to Michael Stoddard of Electra and a much warmer welcome from the other Candover institutions, we finally obtained our £2.5 million from Murray Johnston, Investors in Industry (3i), Robert Fleming, BP Pension Fund, and Electra, as well as Candover itself.

With banking and financial support now secure we just needed to agree the sale and lease-backs. What I didn't fully realise was that when someone says 'yes' in the property world they mean 'maybe'. We were dealing with Commercial Union and Scottish Amicable, agreement was subject to board approval and before their boards approved, a lot went wrong. Surveys revealed two properties with high alumina cement (a fatal flaw) – which were dropped out of the deal – and 8% of the price was held back to cover dilapidations.

Over the next few weeks property funding fluctuated between £30 million and £27 million, but Candover kept an eagle eye on events. Their solution to any shortfall was to subscribe more money and reduce management's equity share. Five weeks after agreeing heads of terms we were no nearer to exchanging contracts.

In blissful ignorance of the way deals work, I set off on a family holiday – a camper trip across the USA from Los Angeles to Miami. I had booked a hotel for the family on Galveston Island to enable me to fly back half way through our vacation, sign the deal and return to continue across the States, but my plan didn't work out. I was pursued by bad news, more dilapidations and doses of high alumina cement. Scottish Amicable lost interest in two of the properties and Commercial Union lowered their offer for others.

I rang home every day, usually from spartan camp site phone boxes at 7.00 a.m. Fortunately, enough good news compensated for the bad; and with sales up and stock coming down the business created extra cash to compensate for the drop in funds now forecast from our sale and lease funding. We had to abandon our hotel; in a catalogue of disasters, Galveston Island was closed by their worst hurricane for years. We pressed on towards New Orleans. At a campsite called Lafayette I rang Roger. The news was not good. Candover's lawyer Ashurst, Morris & Crisp had produced a subscription agreement that was conditional on us exchanging contracts on £30 million of property before completion with Hanson, otherwise the management share would drop. I decided to return home, leaving the family in a soulless hotel in Miami.

After two more weeks of drama and insurmountable problems that somehow got resolved, the deal suddenly changed character. Tony Alexander gave everyone an ultimatum: 'If the deal is not done by Thursday everyone can file their papers.' 'Little problems disappeared and big problems were resolved.' The lawyers stopped raising points and worked through the night to overcome any difficulties. The Hanson deadline created a common purpose. No one wanted to waste three months' work.

The Scottish Amicable deal had to be signed in Scotland. At 3.25 p.m., five minutes before Hanson's deadline, Roger called Scottish Amicable. He reached their switchboard but the extension was engaged. Eventually he got through and the deal was signed with two minutes to spare. At £42 million it was the second biggest buyout in the UK and I had a majority stake in our family business. I rang Alex who took the news very calmly – she always knew we would succeed. She had spent a year with a husband whose mind was thinking of something else and yet it was Alex who gave me the determination to overcome every obstacle. 'Well done,' she said and added, 'at last we can have a proper weekend.'

Having spent so long working in confidence I looked forward to breaking the news, but the publicity following our buyout was an anticlimax. Few turned up at the Friday afternoon press conference near Fleet Street. I was interviewed by an *FT* journalist who gave me the impression that he covered stories like mine five times a week, and when my photograph was taken in Shoe Lane the passers-by took no notice. The Timpson management buyout was hardly headline news.

It had been a dramatic year, and I couldn't have had a better introduction to deal making: I learned a lot of lessons. Tony Alexander taught me the importance of having a deadline, and when Ralph Halpern lost the chance of buying John Collier and Richard Shops due to his brinkmanship, I learned that it takes two people to make a deal.

Although I made sure there were plenty of people to carry on our day-to-day business, I did not give enough thought to what I was going to do when the deal was completed. Understandably, perhaps, buying back the family business was incentive enough, without thinking what I was going to do after I bought it.

I learned to expect the unexpected. Who would have thought that a small mistake would give me the opportunity of turning a proposed 5% share holding into 54%. I learned to be patient with lawyers, accountants and indeed with myself. I discovered that some of the most difficult negotiations were with people on our own side.

Selling the shoe shops

Deciding to sell the shoe shops was the most difficult decision of my life. I was selling the family silver, which I had spent 15 years restoring to the family name. It took six months to accept the inevitable truth and come to terms with reality.

I eventually decided to sell the shops during a flight from New York with Peter Cookson. I was persuaded when we devised a scheme that retained control of our shoe repair business. I knew that we were heading for trouble, although despite our problems we were still profitable. At the time we had a net asset value of over £17 million, including property valued at £8 million.

It was a strange situation; we were hoping, at the same time, to sell the entire company then buy back the shoe repair shops. Before seeking someone willing to buy our shoe shops we needed to rearrange the business into neat parcels that clearly separated shoe shops from shoe repairs.

We put the property assets not associated with shoe shops into a shoe repair pot, establishing a portfolio worth £3 million. The whole company would be offered for sale on condition that we could buy back the shoe repair business for £3 million. With shoe repairs making an annual profit of £450,000, this was a reasonable price and would give our new buyout company a firm financial footing. A significant proportion of the properties could be sold very quickly. These proceeds, plus a strong cash flow, meant that we could acquire the shoe repair business using bank finance and no other borrowings.

Once I had decided to sell, we approached the retail guru and stockbroker Gerald Horner. He gave us an encouraging guide price of £25 million but, despite a few false hopes, he didn't produce a buyer. We followed up leads with Next and Stylo, but all they both wanted was a bargain. After several false dawns, trade rumours suggested the name of George Oliver. Olivers 350 shops were mainly in the Midlands, south-west England and Wales. There was little overlap with Timpson. It was another family business chaired by Ian Oliver. He had recently recruited an aggressive MD, Graham Taylor from Sketchley. Taylor was keen to create rapid growth and we quickly agreed terms: £15 million for the group followed immediately by our management buyout of shoe repairs for £3 million.

It was a sensible deal for Olivers, it improved their profits by putting more shops through one head office and ware-house. I couldn't afford the deal to fall through, shop morale was sinking, trade was getting worse by the week, and sales were down on last year. I was terrified that Olivers would ask for our latest sales figures, but they never did. I spent five weeks waiting to be asked 'How did you do last week?' They based their purchase on figures that were three months out of date.

After a final all-night lawyer's drama – which only ended because their lead lawyer had to catch a plane to go on holiday – the deal was signed at 6.00 a.m. Everyone thought that Olivers had got a bargain because we paid Hanson £42 million for the business and sold it four years later for £15 million. But the figures hid the truth. Olivers bought the shares that had cost us £250,000. My management shareholders each received £750,000 for their 5% stakes and the venture capitalists achieved a high rate of return.

I did the deal in a daze. It was like selling a house you have lived in since childhood, and I was saying goodbye to a lot of people I knew well. I had let them down. The most difficult day of my life was when I had to stand in front of 300 loyal people at Timpson House and tell them I had sold their business. Many would lose their jobs because I had failed to find a way to make our shoe shops profitable. Looking back it was the best decision I every made and to dispel any lingering doubts I only have to look at the shoe multiples who continued to battle on in the high street. Almost every multiple shoe retailer disappeared over the next 10 years, including the dramatic demise of the British Shoe Corporation which had had well over 20% of the market. The ex-Timpson branches helped Olivers survive longer than most.

Some people realised that selling our shoe shops was a good decision, but even I didn't realise how smart it was to keep the shoe repair business. My life changed completely. The deal gave me financial security, with £5 million after tax. It also gave me a less stressful business. The new management team only had to invest £125,000 to acquire Timpson Shoe Repairs. We funded the £3 million purchase price with an overdraft facility from NatWest and, as planned, quickly cleared our borrowings by a combination of property sales and positive cash flow.

With no venture capitalists to worry about we just had to keep the bank manager happy. For me, the sale of our shoe shops was like living through a nightmare, but in retrospect I learned a lot of lessons. Find out when the lawyers are going on holiday. As they will make sure everything is completed before they go, it gives you an idea of the deadline. Be wary of merchant bankers and professional deal makers. It is unwise to put your future in the hands of a third party. Meet your counterparts face to face and do the deal yourself. Watch your body language: don't let the other side know you are desperate to do the deal. Planning the price for our shoe repair business shows that you can manipulate figures and get the answer you need.

Shoetech

For the first time I concentrated on our shoe repair shops, and found them fascinating. A service business is very different from other shops that rely on merchandise: shoe repair shops don't need to forecast fashion; they don't need to invest in a lot of stock; and success depends almost entirely on your people.

It was a completely new challenge. I didn't have to worry whether we had the right boot styles for the next season, or work out how big the winter sale needed to be to clear unwanted stock.

It helped to have clean and tidy shops in the right location, but it was much more important to have an excellent manager and a good team in every shop. If we didn't have the skills, we didn't have a business.

I wasn't satisfied with 150 shops. I wanted to expand. We bought Shoetech, a 12-shop business that had been built up over the previous 10 years. The owners had acquired some excellent sites and their simple shop design, run by some talented managers, made the business very profitable, but they had a management problem: their shops stretched from Cardiff to Crawley. It was difficult to control branches that were so far apart. That is why they wanted to sell.

The purchase was made using shares, not cash – we didn't have any option, the bank wouldn't lend us any more money. As part of the deal I agreed to provide an exit by floating the company within five years. I hadn't anticipated that giving the two Shoetech owners a seat on the Timpson board would cause problems. The trouble was due to our management accounts. The contribution from 12 Shoetech branches represented 30% of total Timpson profit. 'We're supporting the whole business,' said my new directors. The accounts were misleading: as the Shoetech figures carried no overheads, we were not comparing like with like. Individual Shoetech branches were trading well, but that was why I had given up 18% of the equity. Once the rift appeared it was impossible to broker a peace. When Alex persuaded me never to float the company, my only option was to buy my new directors' shares, for which I paid £1.2 million (£100,000 a shop). Shoetech is still, 20 years later, my most expensive deal.

It was worth it, however, as Shoetech taught us how to sell the extra job. Their area manager, Arthur Voller, was an ace salesman – brilliant at converting heel customers into sole and heel customers. Arthur helped to teach Timpson sales-manship, not only the extra sole but also the second key. Acquisitions can bring ideas that help your core business.

I also learned that equity is the most expensive form of finance and to think carefully before letting outsiders join the board.

BSC Shoe Repairs

Early in 1987 I identified a fairly bizarre takeover target. British Shoe Corporation, which still had 2,000 shops and 22% of the shoe market, also ran 35 small shoe repair factories that made a loss. Few at BSC cared about shoe repairs and no one knew much about it. I contacted Chris Marsland their CEO who acknowledged my approach, but told me to be patient. Two years later he was ready to do a deal. I visited all their repair factories twice and knew more about the business than their existing management; then, to establish a price, I wrote a report that was used as the basis of our negotiations.

We bought 35 shops for £175,000, including their flagship concession in Selfridges. As all the shops were in British Shoe properties or Sears Department Stores, we entered into a rental agreement. British Shoe sold a loss-making business and received an annual rent of £350,000 a year. We, in turn, rapidly increased the sales and made £360,000 profit in the first year.

I learned some other lessons: (1) great deals can be done when you are buying from a big company; (2) managers in a Plc don't deal with their own money (an independent retailer often regards his business as his pension fund); and (3) when buying from a conglomerate you will probably know more about the subsidiary than they do.

We spotted a strange, small and very lucrative opportunity, but our approach could easily have been forgotten if I hadn't chased Chris Marsland every few months until he agreed to talk.

Automagic

Between 1987 and 1990 I had regular talks with Mike Strom the Chairman of Automagic which, with 120 shops, was the third biggest shoe repairer in the UK. He could only contemplate a merger that left him in management control. Our talking days swiftly came to an end when we went to Edinburgh and acquired 26% of the Automagic shares from a Scottish institution. We hoped the stake would lead to a total bid but Mike Strom held 47%. Despite a poor trading record, he was able to block any bidder.

Strom's non-executive directors were aware that the business was in fatal decline and in 1992 agreed to sell us 35 Automagic shops, but I chipped the price and Mike Strom blocked the transaction. In 1995 another package was agreed, again for 35 branches, but on the day the contracts were due to be exchanged, Automagic's bank, Barclays, called in the receiver. At a stroke, we lost our 26% share holding and were one of

400 companies that responded when the receiver put Automagic up for sale.

We were advised that most receivers sell for a song, so we offered £1.8 million, we had underestimated the level of interest. When the receiver asked for a serious offer our revised price was £2.8 million. Several companies made similar offers and we were asked to bid for a third time. We had three days to submit our best price. The receiver wasn't bluffing: we thought that Automagic was worth £3.8 million but NatWest would not lend enough money even though I had made a major sacrifice. Totally against Alex's wishes, I once more planned to mortgage our house for £1 million. That mortgage was the most courageous decision I have ever made – because I did not have Alex's support. Having relied on her intuitive judgement on every other occasion, for once we disagreed. I was devastated that she would not listen to my argument because I knew that Automagic would trans-form our business.

Final bids were required for 5.00 p.m. on Wednesday, and by 2.00 p.m. it was clear that our bank would not back a £3.8 million offer. We submitted a £3.35 million bid and crossed our fingers. The receiver promised to call early on Thursday morning. I had a sleepless night and arrived in my office all alone at 8.00 a.m. waiting for the call. It was good news and bad news: our bid was at the right level but an other party had made a similar offer. During the conversation it became clear that we were competing with Mr Minit, our major competitor. Knowing that Minit had almost unlimited cash resources, I rang their Chief Executive, Kenn Begley, with a proposition. I suggested a joint bid. If we were successful my idea was to toss a coin; whoever won the toss would pick the first shop and we would alternatively select shops until the last Automagic branch had been allocated.

Kenn Begley needed the advice of his Chairman. Within 20 minutes my offer was rejected. They said they were determined to acquire Automagic and one day hoped to buy our business as well. I said that with my son already in the business they would have to wait at least 30 years. Thus our conversation was at an end, and the next 24 hours would decide who owned Automagic.

Our team – Finance Director, Martin Tragen, Property Director, Mike Williams, Roger Lane-Smith and me – had to view an information pack in London and fix our final price. With limited resources our best hope was to force Mr Minit to pay a higher price. I was likely to be a bad loser. Roger got to the receiver first and set the rules; they agreed that the sale would be settled by a sealed bid submitted at 7.00 p.m. that evening.

We spent five hours studying new figures which showed a substantial redundancy liability at the Automagic Head Office. By 6.30 p.m. we had not settled on a price but knew we had to offer at least £3.8 million – well beyond our bank support. At 6.50 p.m. Martin went out on a limb – he thought we could fund £4 million. Before we faxed our offer, I added another £12,500 (James said Richard Branson always added a bit extra to avoid being tied on an exact round amount). At exactly 7.00 p.m. we faxed through £4,012,500 and five minutes later we got a reply – ours was the highest bid.

The receivers wanted to start the paperwork straight away. Roger stalled; the letter from our bank was not strong enough to stand scrutiny and he spent three hours thinking up reasons for our delay before faxing through our bank's letter. The receiver gave us an ultimatum. The other party was ready to sign the deal, and if we could not produce better evidence of bank support by 10.00 a.m. the following day, we were out of the race.

Over a late night dinner we made several desperate calls to find the £750,000 needed to bridge our funding gap. Yet, we made no progress. Eventually we went to bed – not to sleep but to dream of how agonisingly close we had been to securing the deal.

The air of gloom started to lift at 9.15 a.m. the following morning with an encouraging call from Brian Ferguson at NatWest Bank in Stockport. By 9.45 a,m. we had his letter backing our deal. We rang the receiver to confirm we had the money and immediately went to their office to start the paperwork. Roger stayed behind but rang me 45 minutes later. 'I have had a call from Mr Minit,' he told me; 'you ought to ring them.' He gave me the number of a room at the Savoy. It was Kenn Begley.

'It appears we are in an auction,' he said. 'Remember the deal you offered yesterday? Let's get together and talk about it.' I said I would think about it and ring him back. I never did.

During the next hour we made rapid progress. Then, suddenly there was a phone call. The room cleared, leaving the Timpson contingent worrying. That final Minit intervention was clearly not enough to stop our negotiations – the room refilled and two hours later I signed the contract with a nervously squiggly signature.

By Tuesday every Automagic branch had met their new area manager and three weeks later the Harpenden Head Office was closed. It was all going well, but Alex was still anxious about the mortgage. Receivership brings all leases to an end. We had bought the business, but only occupied properties on licence as we had to negotiate a new lease with every landlord. Two weeks after the deal I discovered that Mr Minit had written to the landlords of all the most profitable shops offering to pay a substantially increased rent. The danger hit me like a thunderbolt and I thought the worst. I could lose the best performing branches and with them my £1 million mortgage. Maybe Alex was right after all.

Fortunately the licence was enough to protect us and Minit's tactics amounted to no more than sour grapes. The integration of Automagic was swift but it took six months to sell the freehold warehouse at Harpenden for £400,000 (much less than I had hoped for). It took even longer to improve their turnover. The workforce were demoralised, several years of ineffective management had made them suspicious. Lack of investment and a wage freeze affected morale. Customer service and housekeeping were poor and staff dishonesty was rife. We didn't start to win round the workforce until we started to invest. Once they saw that we knew what we were doing, things changed dramatically. Sales increased by over 20% for three consecutive years and by 1998 Automagic supplied 17 of our top 20 turnover branches. For several years Automagic shops have been making us a contribution of over £6 million a year – a fantastic return on the £4 million we paid and justification that I was right to take out that mortgage.

This was easily the most exciting deal we ever did. I learned when dealing with a receiver (or an administrator) that you have to move quickly and be decisive. I also learned never to buy shares from a canny Scot. This was the first time I realised that a deal could completely transform a business.

Within 12 months our profits moved from £650,000 to £2.5 million. I also learned how much business is about people; you won't get the backing of a new workforce until you prove that you know what you are doing and invest money to make things better.

Mr Minit

Once the Automagic branches were converted to Timpson, and life at Timpson House got back to normal, the next logical target was Minit UK, but when my approach to Ian Siddall at UBS got a robust rejection I started to look elsewhere.

I talked to John Jackson, Chairman of Sketchley, about the possible acquisition of Sketchley and SupaSnaps, the dry cleaning and photo processing businesses. After two meetings and three days visiting shops, I decided there was too much risk. I then talked to Angus Mathieson who ran watch repair concessions called In Time in department stores, mostly Debenhams. We agreed a price of just over £3 million but at the eleventh hour they pulled the plug and we went our separate ways.

Within a year of aborting these two deals Mr Minit bought both businesses. The price for Sketchley/SupaSnaps was a modest £1 million, but to secure the deal UDS guaranteed £50 million of future rent liabilities to Sketchley landlords.

Ian Siddall and his Minit team saw Sketchley as a catalyst to create a global multi-service business under the Minit Solutions brand. He launched a major refit, reorganisation and rebranding programme both on the high street and in Sainsbury concessions. The move was a disaster; his management team missed the vital point. Service retailing is not just about marketing, you need onsite staff who can do the job. Minit undervalued their shoe repair managers, many of whom were demoted and replaced by graduates who could not cut a key.

A succession of managing directors tried to run Minit UK, but losses continued to mount and after two years Ian Siddall moved on, being replaced by company doctor Howard Dyer.

Mr Minit was founded in 1957 by Donald Hillsdon-Ryan who opened a heel bar in a Brussels department store. By the time I met him in 1990 to make an offer for his UK shops, he owned nearly 3,000 branches worldwide. After the UBS takeover I made contact with each successive Minit UK managing director and in 2001 got close to acquiring 30 traditional Mr Minit shops, but that managing director moved on before I could do a deal.

When I started talking to Howard Dyer towards the end of 2001, Mr Minit losses were mounting. I later learned that losses had reached £40 million a year. At my first meeting with Howard I was joined by Jonathon Bowie of Bowie Castlebank who owned Klick, the photo business. The idea was that Jonathon would buy SupaSnaps (I also thought of finding out if Johnsons were interested in Sketchley). I soon decided it would be easier to do the deal ourselves and talk to third parties later.

It took 18 months before Howard Dyer was ready to do business, by which time Minit UK had lost £120 million over four years. For months Howard Dyer played a game of political ping pong. He revealed limited information using EBITDA, and concealed the detail I really needed. When he asked for an indicative offer, I responded with a request for more information, which gradually appeared. At one point he offered to sell Sketchley and SupaSnaps without the Mr Minit branches I really wanted. Eventually, in January 2003, we sat down and agreed a deal at £1. He was selling Minit UK (about 750 shops trading as Mr Minit, SupaSnaps and Sketchley). The business came with almost 200 closed shops, but no debt, £120 million in tax losses, and the benefit of some freehold properties worth about £2 million.

UBS were difficult to deal with. I was a little cobbler and they were a big Swiss bank, so they were worried about the £50 million rent guarantee given to Sketchley landlords (I was putting Minit into a ring-fenced company with no Timpson guarantees). They also tried to pass across their pension fund deficit, but that was a deal breaker for us so they backed down. I was determined that my 10-year quest to buy Mr Minit would not be thwarted, and we found an answer to every obstacle UBS put in the way. Despite their arrogance we knew that UBS were desperate to sell, but we also knew we were buying a basket case.

Entrepreneurs are risk takers, but lawyers and accountants are cautious so there are times when it is wise to ignore professional advice. We had to avoid giving any Timpson guarantee over the new company, but UBS insisted that I signed a letter confirming that we had no plans to put the new business into liquidation. Buying a business with 200 closed shops was a big risk; if things went wrong it could have finished up in administration, but I had no such plan. Although our accountant advised me not to sign the letter, I ignored his advice, signed the letter, and the deal went ahead. As a result we bought our major competitor (with the blessing of the Office of Fair Trading) but in the process also acquired 200 closed shops and two loss-making businesses (Sketchley and SupaSnaps).

After closing two head offices and a substantial redundancy programme, we were £2 million in debt. I talked to Jonathon Bowie about selling SupaSnaps but thought his price of £1 million far too low. It cost us a further £2 million to buy out our liability for the 200 closed shops and some other onerous contracts through a company voluntary arrangement (CVA).

The Minit deal completely changed Timpson: we more than doubled in size overnight. The Mr Minit shops were very quickly and successfully converted to the Timpson format, but the rest of Minit UK brought a load of problems. SupaSnaps was declining fast in the face of digital photography, the 120 Sketchley branches were a demoralised bunch, and their 111 concessions in Sainsbury's were based on the misconceived Minit Solutions format.

Selling Sketchley

Six months after we bought Mr Minit, we decided to sell both SupaSnaps and Sketchley. We were already closing several loss-making Sainsbury concessions at a cost of £20,000 for each closure to cover the strip out and redundancies. We sold 30 of these concessions to Persil Services (a venture capital arm of Unilever) but continued to trade the 19 most profitable units.

Jessops, another photo chain, showed some encouraging interest in purchasing SupaSnaps. They offered £7 million and I got quite excited, but soon their price was reduced to £3 million. Before long it was clear that Jessops would never do a deal.

There was only one buyer for Sketchley – Johnsons the Cleaners. Fortunately their Chief Executive, Stuart Graham, was on the expansion trail and when we offered him

Sketchley he took the bait. We agreed a deal at £6 million, which gradually dropped to £4 million and eventually £2 million. Johnson's chief negotiator David Walker loved playing politics – for him, everything was a tactic. Thankfully he dealt directly with Paresh, our Finance Director.

In most of our negotiations a deal is a deal, but not with the Johnson team; they were constantly looking for an excuse to chip the price. When we were close to completion, I was parked in a lay-by on the A49, talking to a Johnson director who agreed that the price was absolutely firm at £2 million. He denied making any such agreement 25 minutes later. We were desperate to sell as the business was losing £4 million a year. The final chip came in the middle of the night when David Walker followed a theatrical speech by announcing they could only pay £1. I rang Stuart Graham to agree. It was a good deal. To be honest, I would have given him £4 million to take the business away.

The previous afternoon, with no deceit or drama, we also agreed to sell the SupaSnaps shops to Bowie Castlebank for £100,000 (I should have taken Jonathon's offer of £1 million 12 months earlier).

After a difficult round of redundancies at Timpson House, business returned to normal. Our management accounts were transformed, and group profits leapt to £10 million – double the level before we bought Mr Minit.

The Sketchley deal showed that selling a business for £1 can make you a lot of money; it also demonstrated the benefit of dealing with someone who knows less about the business than you. It helps to be dealing with your own money, especially when your opponents are playing politics. You don't have to like the people on the other side, but it helps. I dislike dealing with people who are playing a game and don't tell the truth, but the sale of Sketchley was great for Timpson.

Master Cobbler

Later in 2004 we did one small but remarkable deal. We bought Master Cobbler, a 14-shop shoe repair chain in Scotland. Brian McEwan, the owner, had been a Timpson employee 20 years earlier before leaving to build up a good business of his own. Most of his branches were in Scottish towns where we were not represented. I visited them all and liked what I saw. We did the deal over dinner at a hotel in St Andrews fixing the final details over a malt whisky.

The deal was remarkable because the final contract faithfully followed all that we agreed at the St Andrews hotel. Brian and I kept in touch and didn't allow lawyers to come between us. Very few other deals have been so untouched by professional interference.

House Name Plate

The next deal didn't fit into our strategy. House Name Plate, a company based in Wrexham, supplied us with cast brass house signs, and their biggest customer was B&Q. Partners Andy Jones and Guy Tyrell had developed a very profitable niche business which they wanted to sell. They asked whether I was interested and started discussions, but it was two years before we agreed a price – an initial £2 million followed by further payments depending on performance.

I have yet to get my money back; all our other deals produced an excellent return but they were businesses we knew well and bought at a modest price. We didn't know much about house signs and paid a full price based on past profits. We still have a lot to learn.

Persil

One of our strangest and most complicated deals was the purchase in 2008 of Persil Services, a venture capital arm of Unilever formed to develop dry cleaning and photo processing in Sainsburys under the Persil and Agfa brands. It was a concept borne out of corporate thinking and market research – a winner in theory, but in reality a business that never grew fast enough to cover its overheads. We had previously helped Persil Services by selling on several Sainsbury's sites inherited from Mr Minit, but by 2007 the Persil dream was running out of steam.

We were not only dealing with Persil Services; Unilever was in the wings and nothing could be concluded without the consent of Sainsbury. When a third party is involved, life can become almost impossible. We were buying a business from Persil Services acquiring leases from Sainsbury and, at the eleventh hour, negotiated with an administrator who eventually agreed a prepack sale for £400,000. (A prepack is a deal agreed with an administrator before the business goes into administration.) To make money we needed to refurbish every branch and introduce traditional Timpson services, but it took Sainsbury six months to approve our refit programme.

Part of our rationale was to establish Timpson in supermarkets. Twelve months later the Sainsbury concessions were trading well beyond expectation, and we had agreed a major development with Tesco.

Max Spielmann

Our latest deal came out of the blue. In the first week of December 2008 I was with Alex at our house in Wales when Bowie Castlebank went into administration. Bowie Castlebank owned Klick, the photo shop, and had bought Max Spielmann in 2004. They expanded the business at a bad time as the photographic market was changing from analogue to digital. Traditional 35-mm processing sales collapsed and Bowie Castlebank had to re-equip 500 shops with digital-processing pods. From a profit of nearly £20 million in 2004, Bowie Castlebank was making a loss by 2009.

We asked for the information pack and studied the numbers. There were 316 stores but only 87 were fully operating, and in all the other shops the administrator had cut staffing down to one person. Heading for a busy Christmas period, the poor managers were struggling.

We quickly saw that by eliminating their Head Office and shutting the worst shops we could create a great opportunity. Three days later, James and I visited as many shops as possible in the Merseyside area and after seeing seven sites we knew what we should do. Standing outside the Max Spielmann branch in Kirkby we jettisoned our idea of adding shoe repairs and key cutting. 'This business will only work as a pure photo processor and we don't know how to run it,' I said.

'But', said James, 'we know a man who can.' Two hours later we met David Edwards, whom we had met 12 years before when he was running Max Spielmann, which he sold to Bowie Castlebank when Spielmann was trading at its peak. Within 24 hours David agreed to join our project. Five days after the business went into administration I drafted our first offer of £1.25 million for about 150 shops plus 10p in the pound for all the stock.

We visited as many shops as possible and, with the help of their management accounts, decided which shops to buy – but everything depended on having the right team. David

Edwards produced two key members: Jackie Dale-Jones, the field coordinator, and Ivan Sestan, who had been in charge of IT. We met them at a Little Chef near Chester where we spent three hours discussing every branch. Within 10 days we made a detailed offer for 187 shops and, despite the usual last-minute wobbles, the deal was agreed on 19 December – 17 days after the business went into administration.

I only had one worry. KPMG, the administrators, had seriously damaged the business. They had reduced staffing levels, had stopped maintenance, and ceased supplying stock. Sales had fallen by 60%, but the administration meant we had to re-negotiate every lease. In a weak property market we achieved 12 months' free rent, followed by a 30% rent reduction. This reduced their property cost by £4.5 million. Max Spielmann has been cash positive from Day 1, and the 187 branches were so encouraging that within months we were opening more. The final price of £1.3 million included all the stock and the equipment – not only in the shops that we bought but also in those we left with the administrator. We spent £2 million on refits, making the total outlay £3.3 million, and recouped our investment within the first six months. In addition, Max Spielmann has given an extra arm to Timpson – the chance to develop a photo service throughout the group – although I am well aware that we still have a lot to learn about the photo market.

The Max Spielmann deal shows the advantage of being opportunistic. We hadn't even contemplated going into the photo business and yet within 17 days we had acquired a significant share of the market. We are helped by our management style: we went round the shops, discovered the facts, and without bothering too much about meetings made a quick decision. You must be quick with an administration, but I would never have done the Max Spielmann deal if we hadn't renewed our acquaintance with David Edwards. Max Spielmann has taken our business to another level. Profits rose to £15 million.

When a deal is concluded, be prepared for apprehension and anticlimax. The focus of your life has suddenly disappeared, the vendor has also disappeared but he now has your money and you are left with the problems he couldn't solve. The bravado you put into the business plan for your banker suddenly becomes reality. Cost savings have to be made, offices have to close and people must be made redundant.

Don't expect your new employees to welcome you with open arms – they will assume that your management style is just as bad as your predecessor's. No one will believe promised plans to improve the business until you put your money where your mouth is. Despite all this, it is wise to wait several months before you press the spend button. Plenty of people will be keen to create a feeling of insecurity:

'75% of acquisitions are unsuccessful,' said one of my non-executives. 'A lot has to come out of the woodwork,' remarked our Finance Director; 'you should have paid much less.' Then up pops the HR manager: 'Harmonisation of pay and conditions will take at least two years.' Then the area manager: 'My team isn't big enough.'

By simply signing a piece of paper you have changed the business from perfect calm to total chaos. Why do it? Because a vibrant business cannot stand still. And I can't resist a challenge!

The deal dictionary

I have been involved in lots of deals but the most significant is still our management buyout in 1983. During those nine months of negotiation, I discovered a new business-speak, which at first was a foreign language. Here is a selection of my favourite phrases:

Number crunching – Putting forecasts into the computer until you get an acceptable result.

See how they fall – Producing figures without fiddling the assumptions.

Massage the figures – Change the assumptions to get a better result.

Own goal – A deliberate action that unexpectedly does you harm.

Monumental own goal – A classic blunder that scuppers the deal.

Doable – An idea that can be financed.

Will it fly? – Is it doable?

Our game plan – An agreed course of action that we hope the other side have not already worked out.

Get our players in place – Make sure someone is willing to lend the money before making an offer.

Tax efficient – Paying as little tax as possible without breaking the law.

Shelter the taxable gain – Make sure the tax doesn't have to be paid for years and years.

Holding the act together – At times of stress this phrase is useful to keep up morale when no real strategy or hope exists.

The bottom line – The bottom line usually means net profit, but today you can call anything the bottom line. Health and happiness is really the bottom line, but, in our case, getting the deal done is the bottom line.

At the sharp end – Doing something that actually makes money.

Ball park – A figure produced by guess work, often more accurate than anything calculated by accountants and computers.

Let's throw things in the air – We've run out of ideas so let's try a bit of brainstorming.

Can I throw this at you? – Here is my miracle solution, but as I don't want you to laugh it out of court I'm just mentioning it casually to judge your reaction. If it flies (see above), I'll claim the idea as my own.

Just dreaming – A way of throwing this at you with even less confidence. This is the way to introduce a completely wild idea without seeming to be a total fool.

I'll come back to you soon – Don't ring me, I'll ring you.

Let's run it up the flag pole and see if anyone salutes it – We'd better get a second opinion.

I've been to the well before – I'm experienced (and also a bit of a know-all).

It's not my style to say so but ... – A useful phrase when turning down a request if you still want to be Mr Nice Guy.

A white knight that's a sheep in wolves clothing – This is a tricky one, two metaphors should not be allowed. Let's say it means – don't trust anybody.

Pick up the ball and run with it – Do something.

A lick of the spoon – There's no such thing as a free lunch.

Marking your card – Issuing a threat.

Threw it in the pot – Don't change the price, just give me more for my money.

I can see where you're coming from – You've got me by the balls, okay I surrender.

Absolutely – A useful word when sucking up to anybody who's the slightest bit vain.

Take a holiday – A phrase that was once used when companies stopped putting in pension contributions while employees continued to pay their full whack. Recent developments in the pension industry have made this phrase redundant.

I see it as a potential problem – This can mean entirely different things depending on who is saying it:

(a) *An accountant* – I'm desperately trying to find something that may go wrong and there is a slight chance that this may be it.

(b) *The entrepreneur* – This scuppers the whole deal but let's hope it goes away.

A dealmaker definitely needs a sense of humour.

Chapter Five

MAKE MISTAKES

Business biographies don't often mention the disasters. Most of us have a selective memory, bad news is swept under the carpet and soon forgotten. But you can learn a lot from mistakes. Most of the horror stories in this chapter were only recognised in retrospect. I can't claim the credit for forecasting trouble ahead, but I hope I have learned some lessons from my own mistakes and blunders by other companies. No one can be blamed for getting it wrong as long as they don't do it again. Central government's response to any major mistake or disaster is to make a new law to protect everyone against any repetition, but increased child protection, more security checks, financial services agencies and health and safety rules won't prevent further disasters.

Time moves on. Attitudes change and there is no permanent fix to avoid future mistakes. I discovered this truth as a naive 23-year-old buyer assistant, when I wrote a buyers' code. It was a set of rules to avoid future buying mistakes. My guidelines were based on sales from the previous season (which had been a real disaster). My top tips were:

1. Never buy multi-coloured shoes.
2. Make sure that 30% of the fashion shoes are plain courts.
3. Never buy a sling back.
4. Avoid white and beige.
5. Don't buy heels over 2¾ inches.

Next season fashion had changed and the best seller was a beige and white sling back with a 3-inch heel. I soon discovered that fashion is always changing, so you can't create buying rules based on last year's performance – I was showing the ignorance of youth.

Life is not meant to be straightforward: things go wrong, plans don't work, and you get plenty of surprises. So make sure you learn all the lessons. The sharpest part of experience comes from mistakes – particularly those you make yourself. But no one should be ashamed of getting it wrong – in a risk-adverse world it is wonderful to see someone have a go (as long as they don't make the same mistake again!).

Business blunders

Before I reveal some of our own blunders here are a few I have seen elsewhere:

John Collier
In the 1960s there were lots of multiple tailors selling made-to-measure suits: Willoughby, Alexandre, Hepworths, Harry

Fenton, Jackson the Tailor, Dunns, Horne Bros, Hector Powe, Weaver to Wearer – and John Collier, whose demise I witnessed at first-hand. In 1973 after Timpson had been sold to the UDS Group, I was appointed the first and last shoe buyer at UDS Tailoring, which included Alexandre, Claude Alexandre and John Collier. I was there for six months. Most John Collier units occupied prominent high street positions with an enormous ground floor, given over to a big window display and a made-to-measure suit department. Shirts, shoes, socks and ready-to-wear clothes were sold upstairs, but the big business was made-to-measure, spurred on by advertising ('John Collier, John Collier, the window to watch'). Almost 90% of the chain's turnover came from made-to-measure suits.

In those days everyone had a suit for best. Not only was it standard dress for weddings, funerals and church on Sunday, but some people even wore their suit when they went to the beach on their annual holiday. Lots of faithful customers bought a new John Collier suit for Christmas. In 1973 John Collier (previously called the 50 Shilling Tailor) offered three-piece suits at £17.99, made from a wide range of cloth designs. Customers' measurements were sent to a John Collier factory in Yorkshire or the north-east, and the finished garment was returned to the shop ready for collection within a fortnight.

When I joined John Collier, business was booming. There was no hint of the revolution just around the corner, yet within 10 years the made-to-measure suit business had all but disappeared. Rapid changes in lifestyle and fashion created a big demand for a more casual look and ready-to-wear items. By 1988 the John Collier name had completely disappeared from the high street.

While the John Collier team resolutely stuck to yesterday's formula, Ralph Halpern's Burton Group reinvented its business. All Burton shops were refitted, the made-to-measure bar was thrown out in favour of jackets, trousers and shirts sold by self-selection. The team at John Collier was still not stirred into action when they saw Hepworths, the third biggest menswear chain, create their own high street revolution. The Chairman, Terrence Conran, and the Development Director, Trevor Morgan, started a chain called Next, with new recruit George Davis. These new shops made John Collier look even more old-fashioned.

The Next chain was so successful that within five years all Hepworths shops had closed and been converted into bigger Next stores. John Collier reacted to the change with small piecemeal changes to its shops; it didn't realise that a revolution was taking place. In the end no one bought made-to-measure suits and customers abandoned John Collier. The business died because it simply failed to keep up with the times.

Sock Shop

I apologise for picking out Sock Shop as an example of retail failure. When they were first launched by the founder, Sophie Mirman, I thought that her shops were fantastic – a fresh, colourful, brand new concept. I spent a lot of time looking at their displays and copying their ideas. Alongside Tie Rack and Body Shop they helped to create a new term: 'niche retailing'. The press loved this new name on the high street and with an ambitious business plan, Sock Shop floated on the Stock Market at an indecent PE of 40 (or perhaps it was even bigger than that). But once in public hands, Sophie Mirman had to deliver an aggressive business plan to satisfy analysts and institutional shareholders. Her property agents produced plenty of new sites, but at a cost – high rents and big premiums. Sophie needed to produce high sales to pay for the prime sites; shops on Waterloo Station do not come cheap.

Any retail company that expands quickly needs to know a bit about retail property. We turn down about seven out of every eight shops we are offered because they are not right for our business, or simply too expensive. The only way to make a decision is to travel round the high street like my grandfather did in the 1930s. You drive a lot of wasted miles to see the useless sites, but it is well worth the time. You soon recognise a winning pitch when you see it. But growing businesses are in a hurry, especially if the stock market is demanding instant success and exponential growth. Sock

Shop opened too many shops too quickly. As they spread through the country they discovered that a retail formula based in London is not always as welcome up north.

Sock Shop had another problem. Hosiery fashion is cyclical; new products like pattern tights and coloured socks come to the market at a premium price, and customers are happy to pay for the latest fashion. But within months the market gets flooded, prices come down and then collapse. Tights that started life at £2.99 are soon selling at 45p. Sock Shop was launched at the height of legwear fashion; its arrival was perfectly timed but its success couldn't last. Within two years prices fell, sales sank and Sock Shop couldn't pay the high street rents – the business went into receivership and finished up in the hands of Stephen Hinchcliffe (to be discussed later).

Sketchley

Well over half of the well-known high street names of my youth have gone; they have been taken over or closed down. In the past all were super successful – so what went wrong? Once a business has survived 15 years it seldom fails while the founder is at the helm. The problems come when the business abandons its roots, often to satisfy the short-term needs of greedy shareholders.

In the early 1980s Sketchley was becoming one of our biggest competitors. Out of their 600 shops, one hundred had heel bars, run by a dedicated shoe repair team including seven area managers who were experienced cobblers. These shops were taking an average of £1,000 per week on shoe repairs and we were feeling the pinch. Then there was a change in Sketchley's top management. In a move designed to cut costs and satisfy the City by meeting market expectations, Sketchley made the dedicated team redundant and put shoe repairs under the wing of existing Sketchley area managers. They were given an impossible task, managing difficult characters with different skills. Almost 75% of their shoe repair and key-cutting business disappeared within two years, and we breathed a sigh of relief.

We ceased to bother about Sketchley and while we weren't looking they made matters worse – they bought SupaSnaps, a well-run but mature photo-processing chain. In those days all the photo shop business was based on analogue film, which was collected from each shop by courier and processed at a central factory overnight. But big changes were about to happen and SupaSnaps was ill-equipped and unprepared to keep up. The industry introduced expensive in-branch photo labs and moved from overnight processing to a one-hour service, but the SupaSnaps shops were too small for these machines and the investment was too large to be accommodated in the Sketchley cash flow.

Before Sketchley bought SupaSnaps, they made a bid for Johnsons the Cleaners. Johnsons successfully defended the bid and SupaSnaps were bought on the rebound. Sketchley was, at that time, making £14 million a year profit – a figure Sketchley never saw again. Johnsons stuck to the knitting – Sketchley didn't.

In another move designed to create more shareholder value, the SupaSnaps service was moved into Sketchley branches. Senior management was, by that time, run by SupaSnaps people who made sure that the SupaSnaps brand dominated the joint units. When one of the Sketchley area managers took me round some branches in 1997, she showed me their Hitchin shop, where three-quarters of the image was photo, but two-thirds of the turnover was dry cleaning. The purchase of SupaSnaps blew the business further off course.

Sketchley management focused on its share price, the half-year and full-year statements were full of corporate sound bites. In the late 1990s they had to close a number of unprofitable shops, but to camouflage the closure pro-gramme they announced a major expansion with Sainsbury. The Sainsbury concessions were positioned as a strategic move out of town and helped to increase the share price. But the deal with Sainsbury required Sketchley to set up concessions wherever the supermarket decided. Consequently, Sketchley opened lots of loss-making units, many of which were tucked away in quieter Sainsbury stores.

When Sketchley's Chairman, John Jackson, showed me the figures in an attempt to sell me the business, it was too late. They had lost the plot and were led by a team who knew little about Sketchley and its history. Things got even worse when Minit bought Sketchley. You can't save a loss-making business by buying another loss-maker, especially when senior management know little about the business and don't listen to their experienced employees. The history of Sketchley would be a great case study for any business school.

The dot.com disasters

Like many people of my age, I was careful not to openly criticise the fashionable dot.com companies in the late 1990s for fear of looking fuddy duddy. I woke up with mixed feelings on New Year's Day 2000. We had a fantastic party the night before – fancy dress, champagne, fireworks, Auld Lang Syne – but the next day I suddenly felt much older. If the threatened Millennium Bug had struck it wouldn't have been so bad, but it didn't. At midnight the only cloud still hanging over the technological revolution disappeared, giving the all clear for a generation for teenage tycoons to develop e-commerce to their hearts' content. We were faced with a *Sunday Times* rich list full of under-25-year-old nerds with the Queen trailing in 75th place.

On the 1st of January 2000 I finally felt myself confirmed as yesterday's man. But within two months I came to terms with the technology and became rather excited about this dot.com business, and the more money we lost on our website the more enthusiastic I got.

Our website was developed by chance. Every business has its technocrat, who bashes his computer frantically out of office hours; we had Russ, our webmaster, who had previously been shackled as a shoe repairer. At first I didn't understand what Russ was doing. He sat in front of his computer producing no obvious benefit to the business; he might as well have been playing Tomb Raider or Solitaire. Then, one day in June, he proudly presented the first few pages of our website: it showed a map of our shops, pictures of the directors and a page where you could order an engraved house sign.

In August Russ took his first e-mail order, a rustic sign for a house in Harpenden, called Windy Hollow. In September he sold two more; in October we sold a house sign every week, and during November he put more products on the web – pet discs, engraved tankards and shoe polish. In December we sold 14 house signs, engraved a pet tag for a poodle in Auckland, New Zealand, and sold 20 pairs of laces and a tin of brown polish.

This was so encouraging that I asked Russ to coach me on computers. In just four hours he had me surfing the web. I borrowed his laptop over the weekend, but by Saturday night the novelty had wore off and I had my routine read of the Sunday financial press. It was full of e-commerce kids coming to the market at prodigious prices.

I did some research to value our fledgling Timpson.com website. I estimated the total market value of all UK internet stocks at £165 billion. These companies made a combined loss of £1 billion on a total turnover of £2.4 billion, but the analysts said that the current loss was irrelevant, and all would be well. Within three years, the market forecast a profit of £40 billion and my Sunday papers were tipping most internet stocks as a buy. I thought about these figures – to reach a profit of £40 billion e-commerce companies would need sales of £800 billion or £2,000 for every adult in the country.

It was forecast that within three years we would be spending 10% of our hard-earned cash on the net. It might have been possible, but was it feasible? I consulted my daughter, who had been embracing the technology for some time. She went shopping on the web just before Christmas 1999. Needing a costume for the millennium party, she searched for fancy dress and came up with a catalogue of bizarre rubber outfits, not exactly suitable for the occasion. She did manage to buy a book, but it took ages – 24 minutes from switching on to placing the order. Even if I could match her pace, it would take me 12½ working days to spend my £2,000 share of the e-commerce cake.

I showed my analysis to Russ who told me that I'd got it all wrong. Computers double their speed every two months, he said; far from being glued to the screen, the internet will save you time, and you could play even more golf. I walked away convinced that at the current rate of growth our website will be selling one million house signs a week by 2005. Based on Russ's forecast, our website was already worth 80% of our total asset value, therefore I decided to delegate e-commerce management to our under-25s who, in turn, banished me to run the part of the company that makes a profit.

The dot.com boom then bust – it was amazing. In some ways it was more incredible than the bank crisis in 2008. It was pure fantasy; the dot.com companies fooled the stock exchange and even hoodwinked the people who themselves created dot.com companies. Of all the businesses who created a fantasy world and fooled sophisticated investors with their emperor's clothes, perhaps the best example was Boo.com, whose market capitalisation rose even faster than their losses. I won't say any more about Boo.com, because I don't want to spoil your enjoyment of my favourite business book, *Boo Hoo* – an amazing example of how the hype surrounding a new business can fool a city full of intelligent analysts.

British Shoe Corporation

By 1985 I thought it inevitable that a lot of the high street shoe chains would disappear, but I didn't envisage the rapid demise of the dominant British Shoe Corporation (BSC). BSC had been built up in the 1950s and 60s by Charles Clore and Harry Levison. Clore was a genius at property, spotting the freehold value of multiple businesses, buying them on the cheap and using the property assets to fund his future investment. He built up his Sears Holdings retail empire which controlled more than 26% of the footwear market in addition to Lewis's Department Stores (including Selfridges), the fashion chain Wallis, Foster Bros Menswear, Olympus Sports, Millets, Adams children's wear, Horne Bros, Mappin & Webb and William Hill. Clore left the development of his shoe business to Harry Levison, whose own company, Clerkenwell Footwear, became the national chain Curtess. Through a series of acquisitions several well-known high street names became part of BSC; Freeman Hardy and Willis, Trueform, Manfield, Saxone, Dolcis, Lilley & Skinner, Roland Cartier, Cable, Benefit and Philips Character Shoes. Levison developed probably the best buying team that has ever served a retail business. They were so dominant on the high street that some consumers accused them of controlling fashion – which was not true. Their buyers were so good that they predicted fashion better than anyone else had done before or since. When Levison retired in the late 1970s he handed over the management of BSC to Harry Harrison, an operations man trained at Littlewoods. Although Harrison had little buying experience he knew the business well enough to allow the buying team to flourish. Sadly he died within two years of taking over.

The business was then run by David Roberts who was a talented menswear buyer but not such a good managing director. He still had a really large business – BSC was bigger than Marks & Spencer and Woolworths combined, but had reached its peak. David Roberts' successor, Chris Marsland, was an operations man who brought a more systematic approach to the buying department. Flair was replaced by computers, and the buyers – who were controlled by merchandisers – were told how many pairs to buy. It was an unhappy development; some of the buyers left and others were asked to leave. Some of the BSC buying team were in the habit of taking substantial gifts from their suppliers – a habit that was not appreciated by the new management team, especially when sales started to drop. Within two years BSC had lost its major strength, the best buying team in the country had been replaced by a computer.

The new team believed that their market dominance was due to having the biggest centralised warehouse system in Europe, but they had forgotten that the most important thing in a shoe shop is to have shoes that people want to buy. When things started to go wrong in BSC trouble also emerged at the holding company, Sears. After Charles Clore's death it all appeared to go well for a time under the control of Geoffrey Maitland-Smith and Michael Pickard. Then they appointed Liam Strong, the Marketing Director of British Airways, as their new Chief Executive.

I met Liam Strong in 1987, shortly after I had sold our shoe shops. As I was no longer a competitor I was able to offer advice on the footwear retail scene. Strong was in buoyant mood, and suggested that I met Ian Thompson, his new Managing Director at BSC. When I had tea with Ian he told me about his plans. 'It's simple,' he said, 'I'm going for the easy wins.' BSC had just converted one of its shops in St Helens to a new fascia called Shoe Express. It was a concept copied from Payless, a successful chain in the USA, and was an immediate success, which wasn't surprising as the branch in St Helens had been spoon fed with all the best stock BSC could offer, providing every size and colour in all the best sellers. That was Ian's first easy win, and he was going to convert shops to the Shoe Express format as fast as he pos-sibly could. The other easy win was Dolcis, which dominated the young fashion footwear market. For a time Dolcis and Shoe Express produced success, but only just enough to compensate for the deterioration of the rest of BSC. After two years it became clear that Shoe Express was not such an easy win after all.

By the time Ian Thompson had been succeeded by two other managing directors, BSC was in freefall, and panicked. Freeman Hardy and Willis, Trueform and Saxone were sold in a strange hire purchase type deal to Stephen Hinchcliffe, an entrepreneur who had started to build up a portfolio of loss-making shops despite having insufficient financial backing and little retail experience. His chains included Sock Shop and Salisbury's handbags, but the BSC shops accounted for the greatest part of his turnover. Hinchcliffe went bust in a big way and BSC had to take back a large slice of the port-folio. In the end, things got so bad that Sears called in the company doctor, David James (who subsequently conducted the autopsy on the Millennium Dome). James sold the rump of BSC to Philip Green who used it to build a cash mountain for the future purchase of BHS and Arcadia. In five years BSC had gone from 26% of the footwear retail market to nothing.

BSC failed for three reasons, they had not predicted the future of the shoe market, they did not understand the his-torical reasons for their success and, as a business, their culture lacked a moral compass.

Minit Solutions

In Chapter 4 I told part of the tale of Minit and the disastrous development of their Minit Solutions retail format. It was a classic case of top-down management. The idea of a one-stop high street service shop with shoe repairs, dry cleaning, watch repairs, key cutting, photo processing and engraving all under one roof had some merit, but had to be served by staff with the experience to do a good job. I remember visit-ing a Minit Solutions in a Sainsbury store outside Newbury, and asking the girl behind the counter if she could cut my key. 'No,' she said. 'Why?' I asked. 'We haven't had the train-ing yet,' she said, 'but I am on a course on Friday, so I could cut your key next week.'

In four years Minit UK lost £120 million, the concept didn't work and management blamed the staff. 'We have a great formula,' they said, 'if everyone pursues their individual objectives the project is bound to be a great success.' Senior management had fallen in love with Minit Solutions, they couldn't afford the concept to fail. There was a succession of managing directors, but none was a shoe repairer, most of them brought in other people, who also knew nothing about the industry to help them to fix the problem. Area managers came from unrelated businesses such as Burton, Somerfield, Thomas Cook and Dorothy Perkins, none of whom could get their mind around managing shoe repairers. When we bought the business we discovered some of the classic symptoms of top-down management.

To cut costs, Sketchley shops were not allowed to employ window cleaners – so they had dry cleaning shops with dirty windows. The control on costs was so tight that branch staff were not allowed to buy postage stamps. They had to order them from Head Office, who sent them in the post.

Too good to be true

It doesn't matter how many laws are passed, new scams will always keep appearing in the world of business. Box ticking, governance, non-executives and government watchdogs will not be enough to stop the next Madoff, Robert Maxwell or Peter Clowes. Most of us should have been wary of such sharp dealers, but they were plausible, and bankers – afraid to miss out on the next big thing – backed them. That's the problem with bankers who sit in an office, look at the figures and listen to the gossip. They might smell a rat, but if the bank down the road is backing the rat, they will want to back him too. Their biggest fear is to lose out by stepping out of line.

Closer to home

So far I have talked about other people's mistake, but I don't want to give anyone the impression that we, at Timpson, are infallible. Indeed, I have made my fair share of blunders. The remainder of this chapter will concentrate on home-made disasters and what I've learned from them.

Our shoe shops

I am well aware that our biggest mistake created my major opportunity. If the Timpson shoe shop business had flourished in the 1960s and 1970s we would never have had the boardroom row and I could not have done the management buyout. In retrospect I can see why mistakes were made. The business was too committed to the industrial north at a time when mills, shipyards, steel manufacturers and coalfields were being closed down. The new shops were far too small and too suburban and market share was lost to the powerful British Shoe Corporation whose takeover tactics were the winning strategy that Timpson missed (the acquisition of 110 Norvic shops in 1971 was too little too late). But it would have taken considerable courage to go down the winning route and the big investment needed was probably more than the business could afford without taking up big bank borrowings or making a major rights issue that would have turned the family into minority shareholders.

I can, therefore, understand why the Timpson business failed to grow beyond 250 shops and £1 million profit, but I still wonder why I didn't sell the shoe shops sooner. Obviously my sentimental attachment made it very difficult to make a life-changing decision, especially when it meant selling a family business, but I should have been more able to separate sentimentality from business sense. However, in retrospect I take comfort from the fact that I made the right decision in the end and also had sufficient pride in our history and concern for our employees to have a conscience. Good business decisions should not just be made from cold figures, they should also come from the heart.

Keycall

My worst venture was Keycall, a new service for motorists. We wanted customers to sign up, register their key details and, if they lost their keys, a man on a motorbike would bring a spare set within two hours, whether the motorist was stuck in Stranraer or stranded in Stalybridge.

I was advised that direct marketing would soon build a big customer base. A man called Jed insisted that I spent £10,000 on focus groups before investing real money. To Jed, all business could be boiled down to mathematics; carry out quality research, plug in the facts, flex a few probabilities and your return on investment is guaranteed.

Using pure logic, Jed persuaded me to spend £35,000 on leaflets inserted into national newspapers. 'This would', he claimed, 'bring sales of £20,000 in the first year.' 'That's not a good deal,' I said. 'The advertising costs more than the sales.' Jed could not believe my stupidity. 'It's an incredible conversion rate,' he said, 'our research proves a fantastic 0.05 response and you are building a database you can work for years.'

As it turned out, Jed had his sums wrong. Perhaps he put his decimal point in the wrong place; the £35,000 produced a mailing list of just 10 people, including Alex, her cousin from Leatherhead, and two girls in our finance department who were getting the service as a free trial.

Some say that half of all advertising is wasted, but no one knows which half. I now understand how some advertisers waste money. One Sunday outside our newsagent, shortly after pulling the plug on Keycall, I saw a man by a litter bin methodically shaking each newspaper until he had removed all the leaflets hidden inside. I then saw why Jed was wrong and why Keycall hadn't worked. We recorded an exceptional loss of £100,000 and went back to concentrate on shoe repairing.

A lack of humility

When we bought Mr Minit in 2003 we took on an enormous property portfolio which, as well as some closed shops, included the chains SupaSnaps and Sketchley. We knew how to make money out of Mr Minit, but we also arrogantly believed that we could turn round Sketchley and SupaSnaps simply by introducing the magic of our management style. I visited loads of Sketchley shops and saw a business in trouble. Most of the good colleagues had gone, leaving a high percentage of mainly part-time drongos running dilapidated shops in poor retail locations.

Thinking back there was no way we could bring those shops back into profit. We didn't have the management, the time or the money needed to relaunch Sketchley. Whatever we did, SupaSnaps were also heading for disaster doomed by the digital camera. Despite all these obvious problems I was either stupid or arrogant enough to have a go. Luckily within 18 months I found a buyer for both businesses.

Successful entrepreneurs should realise that they have only proved they are good at managing their particular business – it does not mean that they can walk into another company and guarantee the same result. Humility is much more helpful than arrogance.

Timpson concessions

In the early 1980s every clothing shop seemed to be selling footwear. It was a trend set by the Burton Group who offered shoe concessions in Top Shop, Top Man, Dorothy Perkins and Evans. The UDS Group lagged well behind, but eventually asked me to put Timpson shoes into John Collier. Each concession took about £250 per week and made a small profit, and in most locations we let the John Collier staff look after the business. We did more turnover in Richard Shops but didn't make much money because we supplied the staff ourselves. For some reason I couldn't resist opening lots of these concessions very quickly. The increase in our turnover improved our rating within UDS, but the concessions were rubbish. £250 per week was too low to create a proper department and, when we relied on John Collier staff, housekeeping was horrific. After two years the scheme was falling apart. There were empty displays in the shops and unsalable shoes in the stockroom. It was a big mistake – half-hearted measures don't work. I was tempted by random numbers that projected £100 profit a week in 300 shops, making a total of £30,000 extra profit every week or £1.5 million in a year. These sort of predictions seldom come true.

The John Collier and Richard Shops concessions only made a modest amount of money, but they soaked up a lot of time. It was poor retailing: a half-baked offer hidden at the back of each store or put upstairs, seldom seen by a customer. I learned that second-rate attempts to add extra products and services almost always fail, a mistake repeated many times by other retailers. Mr Minit introduced a half-hearted watch straps and battery service that was never developed into a proper watch repair business. B&Q tried key cutting, using an automated machine that never captured the imagination of their staff. When Thorntons introduced cafés into their shops I thought it was a great idea, but they never opened enough of them to make it an important part of the business. Klick, the photo processors, tried mobile phones and Johnsons the Cleaners have had several attempts at key cutting, but neither introduced these extra services with enough authority to make them a permanent part of their business.

If you can't do it properly – don't do it. Don't expand a new idea to lots of shops until you have developed a proper formula. Rolling out a new concept needs to be very carefully handled.

The Free Man Scheme

Our bonus scheme works well; it encourages colleagues to go for extra sales and keep staffing levels down. In the early 1990s I started to think the bonus was working against us. I thought we were losing trade due to low staff levels, but the area managers found it impossible to persuade shop colleagues to take on extra staff. Apprentices were fine because they came at no extra cost to their bonus, but as soon as the apprentice qualified and shared in the bonus pot, shop managers lost out and found a good reason to get rid of them. 'She's a bit slow.' 'George is a poor key cutter.' 'I'm sure Fred will never make it.' To combat the problem I introduced my Free Man Scheme, authorising 75 extra colleagues who would work without affecting the manager's bonus. It was a disaster; turnover went down. With an extra pair of hands available, experienced colleagues took things easy, the buzz went, and we lost turnover. I was paying an extra £17,000 a week in wages and had made matters worse. It took us a year to get back on track.

Theory seldom works out in practice. Don't make big changes until you have tested that they work. Human nature may not be as logical as you think.

*   *   *   *   *

To finish this chapter of disasters here are a few quirky problems that I've seen over the years:

The Chairman's Shoes – In 1975, shortly after Timpson became part of the UDS Group, we were asked to open heel bars in all the UDS department stores. One of the units was in Whiteleys, a department store in Bayswater, London. As this was the nearest store to the home of UDS Chairman,

Bernard Lyons, he sent his chauffeur with a pair of high-grade crocodile shoes to test our service. When the chauffeur returned a few days later he presented the repair ticket, but the finished repair could not be found. We'd lost the Chairman's favourite shoes and they were never seen again.

The Size 4 Problem – In 1969 we had the sort of experience buyer's dream of. We bought a range of corduroy lace shoes from Holland which sold out in less than two weeks. We had a real success on our hands. In 1970 we copied the style in the Far East and I bought 80,000 pairs. Just before I placed the order a discussion group of shop managers pleaded for better labels at the end of each box. It was not easy working in a shop in those days. Faced with loads of boxes, you had to rely on your knowledge of the style number to know what was inside. We decided that the answer was a clear picture on the box end label. I knew that Far Eastern suppliers often didn't follow instructions unless they were given with explicit clarity, so I sent a detailed example of the label to show the size, the style number, the price and, of course, a picture of the shoe. The end result was perfect; all 80,000 pairs were delivered with the correct label and the perfect picture, they all followed my example – every box was marked size 4!

Mystery Shopper – Several years ago, when I was staying at Uppingham for the weekend, I decided to visit Cambridge on a Saturday to look at a possible new site. When I called at our shop in Lion Yard it was very busy, so I had to serve some customers. I showed my lack of expertise by apologising to customers and asked the resident team for help. I didn't realise that one of those customers I served was a mystery shopper who had called to check the quality of our service. A few weeks later I received this comment on my service:

> *I was served by an elderly grey-haired man who was hesitant and lacking in knowledge. I guess he was from Head Office, he got in the way of the other staff who were busy and very professional.*

I was trained as a shoe shop assistant. I have never been able to repair shoes or cut a key, and at 66 it is probably too late to learn. Incidents like this remind me of how much I rely on the skilled colleagues in our shops. Thank goodness for Upside Down Management.

*   *   *   *   *

So that's it, a chapter full of mistakes and plenty of lessons to learn. There's something missing, however. I've been too tactful to talk about the biggest mistakes, because they all concern people, and I have found that almost 90% of all mistakes fall into three categories:

1. Picking the wrong people.
2. Putting someone in the wrong job.
3. Taking too long before demotion or dismissal.

Every Chief Executive makes mistakes. If you play it too safely you'll never grow the business. What distinguishes the good CEO is an ability to learn from experience and admit mistakes, thus gaining respect from his colleagues, confidence from the bank and more profit for the shareholders. If well used, mistakes provide one of the best ways to improve a business.

Chapter Six

CHALLENGE THE RULES

The world has forgotten that management is an art, not a science. If you run a business by the book you will create a healthy, safe and diverse workplace at the expense of the profit-making flair you really need to succeed.

Obeying the rules creates extra cost and guarantees nothing but a mediocre performance. Companies are throwing money down the drain in a national campaign for corporate conformity. I prefer to challenge every regulation in the cause of common sense.

Timpson has only three rules:

two for colleagues in the shops –
   Look the part
   Put the money in the till
and one for everyone else –
   Do all you can to help your colleagues in the shops.

I don't like outsiders telling us what to do. Administrative nonsense deserves to be ignored.

We are lucky at Timpson. Our private business can take risks and follow instinct. Here are some rules and conventions that we ignore in the interests of good business sense.

Salary reviews

We don't have a salary scale. Everyone is treated individually. Their pay is reviewed on the anniversary of the day they joined our business. This is not a cost-cutting measure, a salary scale would probably save us money. We deal with colleagues one at a time because we want to pay everyone what they are worth, giving the good people more than poor performers. Some people think that employees doing the same job should be paid the same money – I disagree. We should discriminate against the drongos.

Salary scales are a cop out; they make the poor performer feel as good as the rest of the team. Scales are usually communicated by a simple circular without looking each individual in the eye.

Our line managers are given a company guideline (usually in line with inflation) one month before each individual's anniversary and they recommend every salary change to

People Support, who normally agree. We encourage managers to be tough with weaker colleagues and generous to the superstars. I'm happy to pay great people much more; they deserve the extra money and I want to encourage them to stay with the company.

Our area managers still spend a disproportionate amount of time with the weakest colleagues, those who need more training and take more 'sickies'. These people make less profit and don't deserve to be paid as much as the trouble-free colleagues who create our success. Individual pay is not a secret. I'm happy for people to know where they stand in the salary pecking order. If anyone is unhappy they can raise a grievance and we will explain why they are worth their current rate of pay.

Employment legislation

In the old days, personnel were responsible for recruitment and training; they kept records, issued welcome packs and dealt with difficult dismissals. Personnel is now called HR and makes sure that the rest of the business stays legal. No one makes a major decision without consulting HR. The HR Director has never had so much power and nothing is left to chance. HR pays big fees to employment lawyers, who cover their backs with cautious advice: 'To be fully protected in an Employment Tribunal we must ... .'

HR departments make management stick to the legislation, and the scales have tipped sharply in favour of employees. Employment law looks after Mr Slow, Miss Sickie and Mrs Miserable.

A few years ago a Job Centre advertised for applicants who were keen and hardworking. They were taken to task and threatened with litigation for discriminating against people who couldn't care less and didn't work very hard. We are proud to discriminate against drongos. We like attitude, we look for personalities with a warrior spirit, and people who care and know how to have fun. Sometimes we get it wrong. They may fool us at interview, but before long they reveal themselves. Here are some warning signs:

— They turn up late
— They throw sickies
— They spend time talking to mates on the phone
— They read a newspaper behind the counter
— They're slow to learn but quick to nip out for a cigarette
— Their girlfriend calls for a 20-minute chat
— They play the fool at training courses

They always have someone else to blame, and whatever they do it's never their fault. One thing drongos are good at is making excuses – 'It wasn't me', 'The traffic was bad', 'Me Mam was ill', 'Sorry I'm not in uniform – someone's pinched my tie'.

We are all playing a silly game. We don't want these people. We don't want jobsworths, moody, idle or careless people, selfish folk that have no interest in our business – these are people who haven't 'got it' even a little bit – they haven't 'got it' at all. The only sensible use of management time is to get rid of them as quickly, as fairly and as neatly as possible.

HR advice, often called best practice, expects us to live a lie. Oral and written warnings plus performance improvement programmes are designed to get rid of unwelcome colleagues. They promise to provide training and support designed to turn absolute drongos into useful members of the team. We are lying. We don't want them to get any better. They might improve their key-cutting skills, but they certainly won't change their personality. Why waste management time on lost causes? It is better to pay them to leave.

We deal with definite drongos with a face-to-face chat and honestly tell them it's not working out – we call it 'Part as Friends'. They don't suit our business and we should never have employed them. If they agree that it's time to leave, we help them to find another job and pay them an extra few weeks' pay in compensation. This off-the-record chat is the honest way to deal with people. It cuts across HR guidelines but, quite rightly, has never taken us to an Employment Tribunal.

There are a few tricky colleagues who are clearly up for a fight. Some love the idea of confrontation and relish going to a tribunal (we have only paid out when we tried to stick to the rules and lost on a technicality). I regard costs awarded by a tribunal as a small price to pay for ignoring stupid rules and treating colleagues with honesty and common decency.

Dictats come from Europe, 100-word regulations are turned in 250 words. HR professionals write more papers on these words, hold seminars and create best practice. Some tribunals find against people whose only crime is to ignore trumped-up guidelines based on namby pamby gold-plated advice.

When we sold Sketchley and SupaSnaps in 2004 we had to instigate a major redundancy programme. Keen to do things in the right way, we gave the task to People Support, who insisted that everyone in the office should be put at risk of redundancy. We should never have let them do it. They sent the letter to people who have been with the company for over 25 years. To suggest they were at risk of redundancy was a blatant lie, but our employment lawyers wanted to hide the truth to look good at a possible tribunal. Never again will I break the trust built with loyal colleagues over many years to satisfy small print in a personnel consultant's guidebook. From now on I will ensure that entrepreneurs run the business, not HR. I won't allow long-service employees to be used as pawns to satisfy a procedural paper chase. I might lose the odd tribunal, but I will win the moral high ground and keep the respect of my workforce.

Appraisals

When I returned to Timpson as Managing Director in 1975, I found that during my absence we had introduced an appraisal system. I went with the flow, but was never confident. Despite training from our personnel manager, I was nervous when I conducted my first appraisal. Probably because it was the personnel manager who was the man sitting on the other side of the table. I felt better when he said it was an excellent appraisal, but I probably gave him more praise than he deserved.

For the next three years appraisal interviews filled my diary. In my keenness to be fair and balanced, I found ways to praise the poorest people and looked for something that good people could do better. I can't remember one interview that brought any benefit and I suspect some did quite a lot of harm. We abandoned appraisals 25 years ago and have survived happily ever since.

For most managers of other businesses appraisals are a big part of their year – 360° appraisals take even more time and create an enormous personnel record. Appraisals are part of a world driven by targets and measurement against best practice, where success is determined more by what you do than by what you achieve. We now let our managers review progress with colleagues in whatever way they wish. Most are in constant contact with their team. Area managers speak to everyone at least once a week (when they phone each branch on Friday to find out the figures and have a chat). Office-based executives are expected to wander round the building every day. Area managers usually have a business meeting twice a year to discuss the detail of every branch with their regional manager. Most managers like one-to-one meetings with each member of their team, but I don't want it to be formalised. Face-to-face praise or criticism shouldn't wait for an appraisal, it's better done there and then with a heart-to-heart chat. Many companies have regretted praise heaped on poor performing colleagues when the file is produced at a future tribunal.

Although we don't encourage formal appraisals; everyone can *raise* problems and *talk* about their future with their boss. Note the emphasis: it's the employee talking and the boss listening. The time we saved by scrapping appraisals has been put to good use, improving the business.

Budgets

I don't waste time on budgets and most of my managers don't even get involved. We leave it to the finance department. Helen Thompson, our Finance Director, gave me a flavour of how we differ from other companies. Before coming to Timpson five years ago, she was in more normal, formal surroundings. She said:

> 'Our budgets take a sixth of the time I was used to. We are lucky, with no outside shareholders and a good relationship with the bank, the budget is not nearly as important as it might be elsewhere. We need a budget to forecast cash flow, but in other companies the budget process is much more significant, it leads to politics and infighting between departments. I've been in places where half the year is dominated by budgets; it's a game with department heads negotiating against each other, making outrageously high bids to obtain the figure they first thought of. No one wants to lose out. They spend every penny allocated, fearing that an underspend will mean that their budget will be cut the following year. It helps that you don't measure performance against budget, you look at last year and common sense.'

To create the budget Helen starts with costs, squeezing them as low as possible. Then she sets the minimum turnover that produces a satisfactory profit. 'The budget is flexible; we may reforecast the figures two or three times during the year.'

Our critical measure is cash. We need to know where we stand at the bank, and we can't afford to have executives playing politics with our money. The budget is not set in stone – it is constantly changing and we can always update our cash forecast. It's Helens job to fix the budget, and she leaves everyone else with plenty of time to make more money.

Management structure

In addition to being upside down, our management structure is very flexible. Classic management structures finish up with too many people: it's a mistake to start with the jobs and then find the people; it is much better to know your people and build a structure that gets the best out of their talent.

We like people who will do two or three jobs at once. We don't like big shots and empire builders. We don't have a marketing department – James does it (I do PR). Mike, who runs Customer Care, also looks after the Postroom, the Cleaners and many other things I don't know about to make the office tick. We like people who like to be busy – we aim to keep growing the business without growing our overheads. Our colleagues write their own job descriptions and pick their own job title. We don't have any employee grades – colleagues build their reputation by being good at their job.

In the field, however, we need a clear structure. Shop managers report to an area manager (who has a team of seven field staff). The area manager reports to a regional manager, who reports to Perry Watkins, who works for James. But if

I find a problem I don't worry about the structure. I simply speak to the easiest person to get hold of. I don't go through the chain of command. We don't work like that; everyone is there to help to get things done.

Whoever picks up a problem deals with it. We don't expect colleagues to say, 'That's not my job.' Dorys, our receptionist, will happily handle a customer complaint, and when Dorys is on holiday plenty of volunteers are willing to run the switchboard. We have a wide range of salary levels but there is no such thing as a pay scale, no pulling rank and no one pressing for the privilege of any position.

If I want advice on watch repairs, I ring our best watch repairer, not his area manager. When visiting shops I arrive unannounced and seldom tell area managers I'm on their patch. I sometimes have long discussions about policy with Perry without telling James. We all know who does what and, more importantly, what they are good at, but I haven't seen a formal management structure for 10 years. I asked Gouy, who runs People Support, and he confirmed that he hadn't seen a management structure either. 'All I can tell you,' he said, 'if there is one, it will be upside down.'

Health and safety

A couple of years ago I sat at a dinner next to a powerfully dressed woman who ran a recruitment agency specialising in the public sector. 'I presume', I said, 'that your success depends on the quality of the people you put forward for each appointment?' 'No,' she replied, 'compliance is top of the list. The most important thing is to do everything by the book and stick strictly to government guidelines.'

Following this conversation I set out to discover whether my business was putting compliance before common sense. I found out that, at the request of our Health and Safety manager, area managers had recently driven thousands of miles to measure the height of every step, both inside and outside every shop. Two weeks later Personnel insisted on another visit to observe every colleague reading and signing a new Contract of Employment.

A few weeks later I visited the Timpson shop in Saltcoats. As I walked in a man with a name badge walked out carrying a clipboard. 'What's all that about?' I asked the manager. 'No smoking,' he replied. 'He's checking that the notices on the window and inside the shop are at the right height and the right size. It is his full time job for the next six months.'

With a chain of shops round the country, most with lethal looking cutters spinning at great speed, we have to take health and safely very seriously. My prime concern, however, is to make sure that everyone is safe, rather than satisfying every jobsworth.

I talked to Michelle, who's been our Health and Safety manager for the last three years.

'My simple objective', she said, 'is to make the company safe by using common sense. I always look for the simple way to comply with regulations without reams of paperwork.'

She went on to talk about her day. 'I've just had a Health and Safety manager on the phone.

One of our shops has left some rubbish blocking the fire exit. He rang to tell me that he's informing the local fire officer who will visit the shop to take action. It would have been easier if the Health and Safety manager had just asked us to move the rubbish (which was removed 10 minutes after he left). He has caused another visit and created a lot of paperwork. Earlier this morning [Michelle continued] I had a problem in Livingston, near Edinburgh. One of our mobile locksmiths was fitting the most basic lock in the staff room of a cinema. Before the job could start, Centre Management required a risk assessment and method statement. These people are not interested in safety; they're just bothered about the paperwork.'

We include Health and Safety skills in our apprenticeship training scheme. Indeed, branch colleagues can pick up bonus points for passing the Health and Safety test. We rewrote all the official safety tips in our own words using lots of pictures. It made the official guideline much easier to understand. Despite all the pictures, we got everything we needed into 30 pages, but we didn't satisfy the Health and Safety inspector, who insisted that the book also included the official version – 53 pages of small print.

It could have been far worse, however. The Max Spielmann Health and Safety manual had 200 pages – every colleague was required to sign in several places to prove they had read the regulations. It is amazing how many people think administration will prevent an accident. In our manual, after the 29 pages that help to make their workplace safe, page 30 is headed 'Bloody Paperwork' – it tells them how to tick the box.

Some companies panic (often under threat of prosecution) and employ a specialist consultant. Once you invite an outsider to become involved you will encounter more nit picking and extra expense. Michelle runs Health and Safety all on her own. I asked her how her department compared with other companies. 'Businesses of our size will have at least five people,' she said, 'but I have the support of all our area teams who help me to make it work. There are 100 people happy to help, so I've really got a big department.'

The power of some Health and Safety departments can cause big problems, because they are allowed to lay down the law and tell other managers what to do. Michelle doesn't issue orders; she helps our area managers to maintain high standards, and it works well.

Planning consent

A long time ago I learned that if you stick to every rule it will cost you a fortune. You can't always wait for a regulator to make up his mind. There are times to take a risk.

When I was running Swears & Wells in 1974 we decided to change the fascias. Half the shops were called Swears & Wells and the rest were Suede Centre. The plan was to convert them all to Suede Centre. Having seen the dramatic increase in turnover created by special sale events following a fire in Birmingham, a sewage flood in Glasgow and a bomb in Belfast, I realised that by closing a shop for at least a week before starting a sale we were guaranteed success. I decided to do the same with Swears & Wells and fixed a 12-week programme of closing-down sales before changing each fascia.

All was going well until our shopfitter found a snag.

> 'We can't get planning permission to change the fascia,' he said. 'It could take three months to get approval.'
> 'What happens if we go ahead without permission?' I asked.

'Well,' he said, 'they could get us to restore the old fascia.'

'That's fine,' I replied, 'probably give us a chance to have another sale.'

We went ahead with my timetable, never applied for planning permission and never had a problem.

Several years ago on a Sunday, while we were holding a children's birthday party, workmen suddenly appeared in the field behind our house. Ignoring a tree preservation order, they knocked down all the trees. They deliberately did the job over the weekend because they knew that the authorities would only appear after the trees had been felled. We would never do anything so illegal, silly or dangerous. We purely act in the cause of common sense.

Most of our shopfitting jobs are so small that we are ready to reopen for business within two days. It can take three months to get planning permission and six weeks for building regulations. It's not surprising that on some occasions we consider the job to be so small that it doesn't require permission. If in doubt, we don't ask.

Similar reasoning can be applied to Landlord's Consent. Many leases have clauses that require you to ask permission to do almost anything. Years ago, we had no idea we would do watch repairs, so it wasn't covered in the user clause of most of our leases. Initially we were only doing a few watch straps and batteries so we decided to take a chance. We didn't ask for permission and very few landlords objected.

Taking risks not only saves time but saves a lot of money. A planning application costs £195 and permission for a new backlit fascia £100. Investigating every approval could add two full-time people to our development department.

But we didn't take a chance when James completely changed our office by injecting a bit of fun. Right in the middle is a fireman's pole – an alternative route for colleagues to descend from the first floor. The inspector raised his eyebrows. 'You can't have a fireman's pole,' he said. 'Why not?' said James. 'It's a Health and Safety risk.' James pulled out his trump card, 'What would you do if we were a fire station?' 'Good point,' said the inspector, who decided that a fireman's pole was not covered by the regulations but could be installed at our own risk. We happily carried out a risk assessment and before colleagues used the pole they were trained in the approved method.

Despite our cavalier attitude, which I repeat is based on common sense, we still get caught by some uncooperative planners. Ten years ago we opened a branch in Canary Wharf. As soon as I saw it I was not happy. It was nothing like our normal image, so I rang Anthony in our shopfitting department to complain.

'Do you want the full story?' asked Anthony.

'Certainly,' I said.

'It's not a pretty tale,' he replied, 'a 10 day job on a 120 sq ft shop took 14 months – it became a big part of my life.'

His story was mind-bendingly long and complicated, involving the endless bureaucracy of London Underground, form filling, shopfitters turning up and then being turned away. It's no wonder that occasionally we question the need for planning permission.

EPOS

Early in my career I was a computer enthusiast. In 1960 I was intrigued by our first computer, which filled an enormous room. It was replaced by a smaller, more powerful machine that the salesman said would 'Reduce stock levels, increase sales and improve margins.' Despite the fact that none of his predictions came true, I wasn't put off. Nearly everyone believed that computerisation was the key to future success.

In those early days we thought computers would eventually answer every problem. The deceptive dream was that they would increase efficiency and save loads of money. I am now ashamed to say that I led the crusade to take the responsibility for stock control away from our branch managers and rely on automatic allocation by computer. I organised the first trial at Urmston and Stretford, branches close to our Head Office. I was visiting the shops twice a week to correct problems created by the computer, but the managers were too polite to tell me they could do much better with a hand-written order.

The allocation system was introduced to all shops. Five years later neither sales nor profit had improved but stock increased by 40%. Not content with distribution, retailers then started to computerise their buying systems. When I was a buyer we did it all – style selection, sales forecasts, stock budgets, size ratios and order quantities. We used flair to place intel-ligent bets on the fashion stakes for the following season. But that combination of experience and intuition was not good enough for the computer age. Buyers were told to stick to stock selection and were given two or three merchandisers (backed by others from IT) who crunched a lot of numbers and placed the final orders, using past trends to predict future performance. But it wasn't always easy to give the computer all the information it needed. Back to School in Scotland was a particular problem.

When I sold the shoe shops to George Oliver in 1987 it was their first chance to manage stores in Scotland. We had a very good children's business, with an enormous peak at back-to-school time. But in Scotland term times are different – they go back to school in August as opposed to September south of the border. In response to the very high sales in Scottish shops, their computer sent loads more stock to Scotland. It arrived after term had started, causing overstock in Scotland and a shortage when children went back to school in England.

As systems progressed we purchased even more powerful technology and our management was expected to change with each new machine. Not every executive wants to learn new tricks. Computers sidelined some great managers in the wake of theoretical improvements. Jack Milligan was one who got caught by the thick end of technology. Jack, who bought our boys' shoes, was an unsung hero who created oodles of profit and rarely received any praise. Without a computer, Jack would instinctively have known how to deal with Back to School in Scotland. He tried, but couldn't cope with a computer printout; for him figures only came to life on the Kardex record he'd been using for 25 years. The business economised by cutting out the Kardex, but in the process killed Jack's expertise. We saved two clerks and lost 20% of our boys' shoe turnover.

By the early 1990s almost every multiple retailer was run by computer, apart from Timpson Shoe Repairs. I only realised the folly of EPOS (Electronic Point of Sale) when we bought Automagic in 1995. Area manager, Tony Sharpe, now one of our regional mangers, told me, 'When I worked with Automagic the computer stock control system caused lots of problems. Instead of placing an order you sent Head Office a stockholding sheet and the computer decided what you needed. But the computer didn't understand the seasons so we got shoe whitener in the winter and weather protector in the summer. We tried to beat the computer by lying about our stock.'

We threw out their 110 EPOS tills and the branch staff cheered. There was no longer a computer telling them what to do. Once again they could order their own stock and even change prices. They felt they were running their own business. Since then we have discarded EPOS from every acquisition – a total of more than 500 tills thrown on the scrapheap. Most outsiders thought we were mad. 'But surely that is modern retailing,' they said.

Removing EPOS has saved us £120,000 a year in maintenance charges, £200,000 in telephone calls and £100,000 in IT wages – that's £420,000 saved by turning back the technology clock. Not only have we saved money, but we now see sales figures two days earlier and have a happier workforce who make us much more money.

Confidentiality

During my time as a shop assistant I was still living at home with my mother and father. One night after they had gone to bed I found some board minutes on the kitchen table. I couldn't resist reading them and was amazed to find that the business was developing a computer system (this was 1960). There was a major investment in shoe repairs and our new Head Office was soon to be visited by Prince Philip. As a mere shop assistant I didn't have a clue what was going on, and I was the Chairman's son.

Decades ago, information remained the property of management. Employees were kept in the dark. We now live in a more enlightened age, but most companies are either reluctant or afraid to reveal the truth. In the information age most facts in the world are available on the internet, but managers still keep company information close to their chest. It is hard to understand the reasons for secrecy, except for facts that are personal or confidential.

Many businesses are paranoid, scared about their information falling into the hands of competitors. There is no need to worry. Company news, plans and ideas are of little interest to anyone outside the company. Most competitors don't understand what you are doing, won't believe your figures and don't know how to use the facts to their own advantage.

For 20 years Automagic watched us develop key cutting. They went into receivership still convinced that we were doing irreparable harm to our shoe repair trade. Despite our well-published increase in profits and market share, some competitors claim that we falsified the figures. We publish the turnovers of our best branches in our weekly newsletter, but seldom find anyone opening in opposition. Executives worry about staff knowing too much. Bad results could affect morale and good results lead to excessive wage demands – it doesn't happen like that. Being open about the bad times gives staff the opportunity to suggest solutions, and good results create loyalty.

When my daughter, Victoria, was living in New Zealand her credit card was close to her borrowing limit and she needed an injection of cash. I rang the credit card company, who told me that the only person who could deal with the account was Victoria.

> 'But she can't get hold of you, she not here,' I said, 'she's in New Zealand. And all I'm trying to do is to pay you some money.'
> 'But', continued the girl at the other end of the phone, 'I can only deal with your daughter.'
> 'Could I have a word with your supervisor?' I said. When she came on the phone I got the same story. I decided to use a different tactic, 'If I sent you a cheque for £500 would that clear the account?' I asked.
> 'No,' she replied.
> I was getting somewhere. 'If it was £750, how would that do?'
> 'Getting close,' she said.

'I'll make out a cheque for £1,000 and send it to you today.'

'That would be perfect,' she replied.

At last I'd found someone who didn't allow confidentiality to get in the way of common sense.

Some people are paranoid about picking up the phone, they are terrified to talk to someone who has not already been screened by their PA. We, on the other hand, are very happy for everyone who works for us to have our mobile number and, if a journalist comes on the phone, I take the call straight away. Journalists need news and are more likely to give a good press to people who help them to get it. Sometimes, however, it goes wrong. From time to time you can expect to suffer at the hands of a sharp newspaper reporter, but it is worth the risk. I can only remember two interviews I regret over the last 25 years.

I can't see the point of keeping things secret. Telling everyone what's going on and how they are doing is a great way to motivate. Just like The John Lewis Partnership, we publish sales figures in our weekly newsletter. Although I don't have to do it, I produce an annual report so that everyone knows how much money we make and how we make it. At every area managers' meeting I talk through our strategy. I don't want colleagues to get any surprises; it's much better to tell everyone about our intentions while the future plans are being formulated.

When I started sending each branch manager details of the profit and loss of the shop in which they worked, colleagues thought I was mad. 'When they see how much their shop makes they'll want more money,' they said. It has never happened. Knowing that their branch is very profitable gives a sense of job security.

I don't just give our information to colleagues, I also tell our suppliers, many of whom depend on us for their livelihood. At our annual Suppliers' Lunch I reveal the latest profit figures, outline the headlines and tell them about our future plans.

If I was sensitive about confidentiality I could not have written this book, which reveals every detail about the way we run the business. I am happy to tell our secrets because I'm proud of what we have achieved, but very few companies will have the courage to copy what we do.

Governance

A new principle seems to have popped up in business – governance. Best practice, risk assessment, due diligence and legal advice all fit in with this new phenomenon. The idea is that no entrepreneur should make a decision without seeking an expert second opinion, usually from a consultant or an accountant. If that opinion differs from his own, he is, by definition, ignoring best practice and taking an unnecessary risk.

Can I just make it clear to Whitehall, the City, academics and consultants that you can't run a business by following a set of rules. If there was a simple formula that always worked we could leave the running of our companies to accountants, consultants, corporate lawyers and even to civil servants. But it just doesn't work like that. Every rule and every box they tick in the cause of caution has been designed to solve yesterday's problem and stop last year's mistake.

The Children Act didn't do any good for baby Peter in Haringey; auditors were no help to Madoff's clients; and governance carried out by non-executives at Northern Rock failed to divert disaster.

All the governance the government has thrown at us fails to stop future failure. I learned some economic rules at university, but as soon as I started to run a business I discovered that economics is an art, not a science. Please don't think I'm a cavalier character who takes irresponsible risks; in fact I am prone to be paranoid. I check our bank balance every day and listen carefully to my non-executive directors, but I can't see why I have to pay professional fees for advice I don't need.

I was surprised a few years ago to find that we were spending money on legal fees in respect of customer complaints. The person responsible put forward the defence, 'When the complaint comes in a lawyer's letter I wouldn't be doing my job if I didn't seek proper advice.' 'But', I replied, 'these lawyers are doing your job for £150 an hour.'

The same thing was happening when we were sued for accidents at work (usually white finger, contracted by an employee who left the business 30 years ago). These claims normally come from the no-win, no-fee market.

'Why do we refer these claims to lawyers?' I asked.
'No choice,' came the reply. 'The no-fee solicitor told us to contact our lawyer. I had to protect your interest.'
'I wish you'd told me,' I said. 'Half of these people are rogues.'

The Pensions Regulator seems paranoid about conflict of interest and doesn't trust the owner and director of a business to look after the interests of its employees and pensioners without seeking third-party advice. Perhaps they don't appreciate that there are companies like ours that run a pension fund for the benefit of the employees. It's our way of rewarding the people who give us the most loyal service. We are not all like Robert Maxwell!

Most governance misses the point. It concentrates on making sure that organisations follow the prescribed method rather than helping them to achieve the right result. There are few areas more stupid in this respect than in employment, where nothing much matters apart from the paperwork. We had one person who claimed unfair dismissal; he was a poor performer but because the area manager knew he was likely to be tricky, we followed the disciplinary process in detail but, sadly, put the wrong date on one of his letters. That error would have lost us the case, so we settled before it came to a tribunal.

When we were selling Sketchley and SupaSnaps, Gouy, our Personnel Director, told me that we would have to consult with all staff 28 days before doing the deal. He was only telling me the law.

'You must be joking?' I said, 'I can't go public before we sign, the other side will have me over a barrel.'
'But it's our legal advice,' Gouy replied.
'The business', I said, 'is not a bureaucracy, we are paid to take risks and that includes deciding when to ignore advice.'

Somewhere along the way we have lost the plot and process has become more important than the end result. Perhaps one day the world will realise that governance does not create success, it simply covers the backsides of people who fail.

Box ticking

Box ticking is bad for business. A company that is controlled by a collection of KPIs should not be surprised when they discover that their people modify their behaviour purely to produce the result their master is monitoring. For me the only KPIs that matter are: turnover, profit and cash. Everything else is a means to an end and should never be an end in themselves.

Of course, like all businesses, we have been guilty of box ticking. When we had 'mystery shoppers' who completed written reports, they followed a checklist. One question was: Did the assistant talk to you? (It contributed 5% of the total score.) I spotted one report that awarded 5% for saying something, but on the line below, in answer to the next question (What did they say?) the 'mystery shopper' entered: 'p*** off'. We have replaced this box ticking with mystery DVDs. The mystery shopper is now a walking tripod, carrying a hidden camera. No report is written, we simply show the resulting DVD to the person being filmed and let them draw their own conclusions. It works much better.

One day I went to an employment tribunal that had nothing to do with us, I was purely an observer expecting to see a court bending over backwards to turn a half-baked claim into a big pay day for a third-rate employee. I was in for a bit of a shock. The employee, a small man called Lee, arrived with his mother – he had no lawyer. Three managers from the sweet factory followed with their solicitor carrying several files. As the note-taker took her seat and the usher checked that all was in order, three men came through a different door and sat on big chairs behind the top table. On the left, a beard with a Lancashire accent, on the right, club tie and blazer and in the middle, the Chairman with half glasses.

Lee's immediate boss, a tough Lancastrian lass called Carol, was the first to give evidence. The bench looked on in awe as she quoted from a 200-page dossier (called the Bundle), which charted every word that led to Lee's dismissal. The facts were fairly simple – just after Christmas the factory was quiet so Carol asked Lee to abandon his liquorice allsorts machine and do a bit of packing. Lee refused (probably thought packing was women's work), claiming he had never packed during his six years at the factory, so had no training or Health and Safety briefing. Lee was suspended. Later when he stubbornly refused to ever work in packing he was sacked. Carol's boss took the stand and, quoting from the same Bundle, proved that Lee was suspended according to the book. Then Pete, the general manager, described Lee's appeal and final dismissal. The sweet factory team were well rehearsed, their solicitor prepared them well and provided every pertinent piece of written evidence, including Lee's job application, their health and safety policy and the Company Handbook, with a form that Lee had signed to confirm that he had read and understood every word.

When Lee took the stand it was like a 24-handicap golfer playing against Tiger Woods. From the bench, Club Tie tried to help him, but Lee made the mistake of speaking his mind. 'I feel victimised,' he said, 'packing didn't require my talent.' But', said The Beard, losing patience, 'you signed their handbook and accepted the working conditions.'

The solicitor summing up for the confectionary company pointed out that their paperwork was immaculate and Lee was sacked according to proper process. Lee's closing remarks were short and not particularly to the point. The Chairman announced that he would sum up after lunch, but I left, but Caroline from People Support waited for the verdict. She saw me later that afternoon. 'Lee lost,' she said, 'I think it was harsh, but it shows the importance of perfect paperwork.' 'Yes,' I agreed, 'the only winners were box ticking and red tape.'

In the early stages of our deal with Mr Minit, we had signed the confidentiality agreement but they sent us very patchy information. After three weeks they agreed to give us the list of branch addresses and total turnover for the previous year. The information came by e-mail but someone pressed the wrong button and, as a result, we received their detailed branch accounts for the last two years, which was just the information we needed. After 24 hours they realised their mistake and made a request, 'Could you e-mail us, to confirm that: (a) you have not read the figures we sent you; (b) you have deleted our e-mail; and (c) you have destroyed any hard copy you might have made.' I have always regarded myself as being particularly honest and above board when doing a deal, but I'm not that honest. That request could only have come from a lawyer.

However much you disapprove of the practice or dislike the task, you won't be able to avoid box ticking, so the best way round it is to appoint a person to do the box ticking for you. This will leave you to get on and run the business using your conscience and common sense. I hope that one day someone will see the light and put a stop to all this nonsense.

Business plans

Recently I was clearing out some files, when I unearthed our shoe shop corporate plan for 1985. The management team had compiled the document during a two-day retreat at Stratford on Avon. It was an early example of joined-up thinking. We believed that if we all aimed for a common goal, success was assured – but it didn't work. The presentations were full of political posturing and the five-year forecast was an extrapolation of dreams that could never become reality. Within 18 months the business was performing so badly that I sold it.

By 1990 retreats were unfashionable and companies called in consultants to do their planning as they thought it would save management time – but it didn't. A local food manufacturer's senior team was tied up for weeks talking to their consultant. When his thick report turned up it told everybody things they already knew, and perhaps the least surprising conclusion was that the consultant should stay on for a further couple of years. As sales and profits plummeted the management team was booted out and the new team appointed a new consultant.

Corporate planners make it sound so feasible. Let's look at the structured approach to planning that I saw in one consultant's brochure:

1. Identify the right financial information and the best format for easy assessment.
2. Develop KPIs and benchmarks to drive performance.
3. Define a process for approving and reviewing marketing plans.
4. Improve reporting and evaluation of marketing initiatives and campaigns.

It describes a future based on quality thinking which will eliminate risks, but business plans fail to take account of flair and never recognise the paramount importance of people.

Despite my misgivings there are times when you need a business plan to show to the bank, or, when necessary, to potential investors – it's the first thing they look for. Make sure that you provide four vital ingredients:

1. *Bring the plan to life with pictures.* The pictures provide bankers with the first-hand knowledge they crave without forcing them to leave their London office.
2. *Find several reasons to support a substantial sales increase.* You don't need to believe your sales plan, just make sure it sounds plausible to a 27-year-old City wiz kid.
3. *Find some substantial cost reductions.* Most accountants and bankers regard cost cutting as the only way to increase profit.
4. *Make sure sales increase so much faster than costs, profits will more than double.* The figures must be so indecently optimistic that they can cope with any sensitivity analysis and help the prospective bankers to declare your proposal totally robust.

By now you must think I am cynical about business plans but you will be amazed to discover that I occasionally do my own bit of planning. I call it strategy. Every six months, without any help from a consultant, I sit down with an A4 pad and try to answer two questions:

1. What will we be doing in five years' time?
2. How will we get there?

A few quiet hours' contemplation can get the thinking straight. I don't delegate planning to my management team or an outside consultant. Strategy is my job.

*   *   *   *   *

We manage our business successfully without having rules. We resent outsiders who tell us what to do, especially when we don't understand the reason for their regulations. From time to time someone says, 'You can't do that,' and I ask, 'Why?' The answer comes, 'It's the law' or 'No one else does it.' Things that work for other people may not be right for us; you make money by taking risks and being different. If we followed the herd we would make mediocre profits.

— 'But it's best practice,' they claim.
— 'Who says it is?' I ask, and usually the answer is, 'A consultant.'

When they say 'It's the law', be careful. Dig deeper. Is it really the law? Can they show you the legislation? I look at the Act of Parliament, and 75% of the time the so-called 'law' doesn't exist. These consultants are talking about a recommendation from another consultant. Even if it is on the statute book, is it a law worth following? Sometimes the law is an ass, and if the penalty is not too severe, it is well worth ignoring some rules in the cause of common sense.

The more rules you bring to your business the more complicated it gets. I believe in keeping life simple and there's nothing simpler than being guided by common sense. Be wary when someone starts using technical terms you cannot understand. When I've been faced with a team talking a strange language full of techno speak, I've usually found a fundamental problem lurking behind the buzz words. Perhaps they are enjoying the technology but don't realise they also have to make a profit or, much worse, they are simply trying to keep you at a distance. Whatever the reason, clear a space in your diary, break into their world and keep digging until you can translate the jargon into simple words you can understand. You'll probably discover that what they think is a technical problem is simple to solve.

Rules and regulations are invented by people who think that the best way to manage is to issue orders from the centre. No one can control the detail by rules from Head Office or laws made in Brussels. Every entrepreneur should be prepared to challenge the rules in the cause of common sense.

Chapter Seven

SURVIVE THE STRESS

Business is a mind game. Entrepreneurs need enough self-confidence to gain the respect of their team and take the risk needed to make money, but they mustn't be arrogant. Pride really can come before a fall. It's a lonely life at the top of a company and Chief Executives can find it difficult to judge their own ability. An optimist is never as good as he thinks he is, and a pessimist is never as bad. When colleagues shower you with compliments you can't be sure whether they are telling the truth or if their friendship is a ploy to help future promotion. The excitement that comes with your original appointment may change into apprehension once you realise that the buck stops firmly at your desk.

If you take charge of a successful business, you will be judged against your predecessor. It is better to take charge of a business in trouble. For 12 months there will be plenty of people from the past to blame. But your honeymoon won't last very long. Eventually the company will face problems that were caused on your watch, and the real test comes when there is no one else to blame. This is when many Chief

Executives discover a new side to their personality – self-doubt can creep in and quickly lead to stress.

I first met up with stress in 1976, but in those days you didn't talk about it in case you were labelled as a person who buckles under pressure and can't take the strain. The stigma makes things worse. You try to hide your affliction by working harder just when your body wants to take things easy.

When I started running the shoe business nothing seemed to go wrong. For six months I was an unqualified success. Then, suddenly, I lost confidence. I began to wonder whether the success story of my dreams would ever happen, and realised that I wasn't so clever after all. Within a week, lingering doubts about my ability had turned to despair, and everything changed. I couldn't concentrate for more than two minutes, but at the same time I couldn't stop thinking about the business. Half of the time I was nervous and twitching, and for the other half I felt depressed. I became forgetful. Once I completely forgot an appointment to play squash – a simple slip that further undermined my confidence. I stopped planning ahead. There was no desire to face up to the future, I was irritable and bad tempered – the fewer people I saw the better, so I didn't arrange any appointments.

For six weeks I hid my problem from everyone, not just at the office but also at home. Eventually Alex detected a change of mood and sent me straight to the doctor. Anti-depressant pills helped a bit, but the talk with Dr Angus Luscombe helped much more. He explained how stress is caused; that it's the body's way of saying 'enough is enough'. Too much adrenaline and tension will in the end produce a breaking point. When he told me that the feeling would soon disappear, I didn't believe him, but he was right. Three weeks later everything was back to normal, but before long it reappeared.

One day I set off for London full of confidence and then, for no reason at all, I returned home in the depths of despair. I had nothing to worry about, so why should I be worried? I ignored the problem, thinking it would go away, but it didn't – not until I returned to see Angus Luscombe. I had learned a lesson – you can't beat stress on your own, so never be too proud to ask for help.

Fortunately I've never had severe stress when it really mattered. The adrenaline of a big deal somehow keeps you going with no time left to worry. It's the little things that knock my confidence – missing an appointment, giving a poor speech or losing my mobile phone have all been enough to trigger it off.

I still have bad days, but at least I know what to do. As soon as I recognise the signs I tell those nearest to me (Alex and Christine, my PA) that I am not on top form. I know it won't last forever, but when you're depressed time passes so slowly that a day seems like a week, and a week seems to last forever. If I'm no better after 10 days I go back to the doctor and do exactly what I'm told. I've learned to be patient: unexpectedly the tension will ease and before long it will be completely forgotten.

Stress makes you irritable but teaches you to be more tolerant of others with the same problem. Many more people are affected by stress than care to admit it. In this chapter I want to be frank about my experience in the hope that it might help someone else.

As I've grown older, stress has become less of a problem. Perhaps the business has fewer disasters, or maybe James now deals with the day-to-day difficulties that used to get on my mind, but life is still not stress free.

Silly mistakes

A few years ago I had a really bad day at the office. We were gazumped on a deal I had worked on for months. Then I missed a meeting about watch repairs that I had desperately wanted to attend – I'd put the wrong date in my diary. Even so, I remained calm until, on the way home, I filled my car with unleaded (it should have been diesel). Two hours later, as the car was towed away, I got my first hint of depression, the twinge that announces oncoming misery like the first sign of flu. When I awoke the following morning I dreaded facing the busy day ahead, and could not get that petrol pump out of my mind. Suddenly our business, which had looked so full of promise, was beset with problems which I turned over and over in my mind, but couldn't come to any conclusions.

I normally enjoy chatting round the office but that day other people were just a pain. I tried to look interested, but couldn't fool Christine. 'Are you all right?' she asked.

'Just a lot on my mind,' I replied. 'Could you cancel my meetings in London on Thursday? Tell them its pressure of work.'

Alex was waiting when I got home. 'I've been speaking to Christine,' she said. 'She says you're bad tempered, and it's your fault. You do far too much. A conference speech in London, golf goodness knows where, and then you leave at 7.15 a.m. to play tennis. Who do you think you are? You are nearly 60. You know where to go to get help.'

The next morning I went to the doctor and the receptionist greeted me cheerfully: 'You look well,' she said. I tried to smile, realising that my depressed state was well camouflaged by a healthy golf course tan. I waited for half an hour looking at last year's *Cheshire Life* but not reading a word.

The waiting room was so full of ashen-faced people that I wondered if I should face my problem on my own and not waste the doctor's time.

Exchanging my prescription for a packet of happy pills at the pharmacy made me feel a whole lot better, but I was still miserable the following morning. I dreaded yet another day surrounded by superbly confident colleagues, whose decisiveness put me to shame. Just thinking about them made me tired. I took a day off and even started to talk about retirement, but Alex quickly changed my mind, 'Now I know there's something wrong with you,' she said. 'If you spent your life at home you'd be bored out of your mind.' She was right. Within a few weeks I felt much better and thoughts of retirement had completely disappeared.

The recent recession has caused an enormous increase of stress in the boardroom. All business leaders have had plenty to worry about. It is difficult to live with the responsibility for a loss-making business. It is even more difficult when you know that within days you must make several colleagues redundant. Also, it is desperately frustrating to face a stubborn bank manager who puts prudent lending rules ahead of commercial common sense.

Conscientious Chief Executives are constantly turning business problems over in their minds. To the irritation of friends and family, they become absent minded and bad tempered, and their life is so dominated by business that they can become ineffective workaholics. Stress can turn an extrovert into an introvert overnight; it can cause a family breakdown and has ruined many careers. People who sail through life without a care in the world, don't help. 'Don't worry,' say some, or even worse, the horrible remark, 'Cheer up, it may never happen.'

There is no way to completely avoid stress, but some things can help. I list a few here in the hope that they will help other pathetically paranoid CEOs who sometimes wonder if their self-confidence will ever return.

Don't keep it to yourself

The first time you sense the symptoms of stress it all seems weird and quite disturbing. You feel unable to concentrate and you are constantly turning seemingly insoluble problems through your mind. You alternate between butterflies in your stomach and feeling miserable, hoping each morning that you will wake up in a carefree mood only to find that you are already wandering from one problem to another while brushing your teeth.

It is natural to hide your mood swings. You are surrounded by cheerful people asking 'How are you?' or 'How's it going?' You reply 'Great,' but you're feeling even more miserable inside. While you are worried, the rest of the world hardly notices. There is some sense in your natural wish for secrecy as stress makes you feel vulnerable and fearful of ridicule, living in dread of people who are quick to criticise. Keeping your problems bottled up inside, however, simply makes things worse. You need to talk, but it's unwise to tell everyone you've lost confidence, or announce your anxiety in a weekly newsletter. Talk to the people closest to you – your partner, your PA and, if you have one, the non-executive director who acts as your guru. They will be relieved, because they almost certainly will have noticed your mood and have been waiting for the right moment to ask what is wrong.

Those closest to you suffer most; you hide your emotions from the rest of the world, but quickly lose your temper at home or in the privacy of your office. Bring those people who matter most into your confidence as they deserve your trust and, in return, will give you the help and understanding you need.

Visit the doctor

I thought that taking my first anti-depressant pills was degrading. I hid them in my briefcase and only popped them into my mouth when I knew no one else was looking. But I needed that help; they calmed down my constant worry and gave me enough confidence to start on the road to recovery. Deciding to go to the doctor, ringing to make an appointment, and turning up at the surgery were indications that I was keen to help myself. Although I originally thought that seeing a doctor was an admission of defeat, I later saw it as the first sign that I was going to get better. My attitude to stress and depression has improved since I collected my first prescription in 1976, but there is still a long way to go. The way Gordon Brown's ability was questioned in 2009 shows that political journalists still regard even the *suggestion* of stress as an unforgivable weakness. By going to a doctor you place yourself in the hands of an expert as doctors see anxious patients all the time. They not only know the symptoms but also know what to do, and you quickly realise that you are not the only person in the world who suffers from stress.

Take exercise

Most doctors recommend exercise as the perfect partner for pills. Although I prefer competitive sports like tennis and golf, I find that the best way to relax is to go running. Don't choose golf as an anti-depressant; the exercise is too pedestrian and the game itself can be stressful. Running worked for me because it cleared my mind. After a few minutes on the road, I was finding solutions instead of constantly thinking of my problems. I stopped jumping from one thought to another and enjoyed a period of concentration. Runners can enter a world of their own where no one can interrupt them. It's almost impossible to use a mobile phone and I've

r found a need for an iPod. A solitary jog creates a
ceful haven. Strenuous walking, swimming, horse riding
or cycling all have the same effect and are much better ways
of having 'a break from work' than sitting with a book, with
nagging problems always going through your mind.

Clear your desk

If your office has piles of paperwork and unread magazines,
throw them all away. Their very presence is a cause of
concern – proof that you're not on top of the job. Most of
them aren't worth bothering with, if they were important you
would have read them. Get rid of the worry by putting them
in the bin, they will never be missed.

Some people – my PA Christine, for example – like to be
surrounded by a mountain of paper. I thought she was the
exception until I did a tour of the office a few years ago.
My Property Director had used all the available shelf and
desk space in his office and was piling paper on his floor.
'A lot going on right now,' he explained; 'these files all relate
to live issues.' My Personnel Director had no files on his
floor; his thing was to keep back numbers of management
magazines neatly arranged in four-foot skyscrapers. My
Finance Director was not particularly tall and it was difficult
to see him behind the mound of paper on his desk. He was
compiling a board report on paperwork savings – I didn't
ask the obvious question. I was nearly fooled by our Training

Manager whose desk was totally clear apart from a proud display of training manuals, but he keeps his office paper-free by stuffing everything into 15 filing cabinets.

One office was a big surprise. When James lived at our home you could hardly get into his room for clutter, but on my tour of inspection his office was a paper-free zone. James told me the secret. 'I have a simple rule,' he said, 'I only look at things once; after reading a document I throw it away.' And he was throwing things away in some style, using a large cardboard carton as a waste paper basket. (On top of his carton I noticed the screwed-up remains of a useful note I had sent him that morning.)

We saw the ultimate paper-free office when James and I visited the cleaning company, Sol, in Helsinki. Their head-quarters is a converted film studio, with stylish graffiti and life-size comic sculptures of Liisa and Reijo, the owners, watching everyone at work. But a lot of the staff weren't there; they could come and go as they pleased. 'It's the end result that matters,' said Liisa, 'not where the work is done.' Centre stage was a coloured Wendy house for private meetings, the rest was hot-desking with no paper allowed.

James was so impressed with what he saw that he has completely refurbished our office on the same lines. I hope the lack of clutter will help our colleagues to clear their minds, but Christine will still be surrounded by paper. As she keeps cool at all times, I'm letting her do exactly what she wants.

Do it now

Save yourself a lot of trouble by doing every job immediately. Two big causes of stress are a mounting workload and a lousy memory. 'Do it now' avoids both of these problems; you don't forget to do things if you do them straight away.

Alex passionately hates my BlackBerry, but it has been a major factor in reducing stress. As soon as something crops up I can send an e-mail; if I get a message, I send an immediate reply. Some people say it is bad to take your BlackBerry on holiday, but I disagree. Thankfully, I have never become attached to a laptop, which I understand is like having the office with you wherever you go. My BlackBerry comes with me (hidden from Alex in my wash bag) and as I deal with e-mails every day, I know I am not returning home to any surprises. Five years ago (pre-BlackBerry), going through all my messages after two weeks away was seriously stressful, but now I don't have to worry.

It's an education spending a day out visiting shops with James; he is an expert at 'Do it now'. If he sees a possible property to rent he takes a picture and sends it with an e-mail to Tricia, our Property Director, while still standing in the street. If we spot poor housekeeping the Area Manager has been phoned before we are back in the car. Another colleague has a problem: his car has broken down and he can't afford to put it back on the road; he needs a hardship fund loan and it's organised before we arrive at the next shop. If James gets an e-mail from our bank manager who wants to meet up, a date will have been arranged within 10 minutes. It's so obvious. I don't know why more people don't 'do it now', but most people repeatedly find reasons for putting things off.

One day, I dropped into one of our management meetings. The minutes of the last meeting showed executives' initials in the margin where action was required. George, a lifetime administrator, had his initials everywhere. George had done nothing, but had an answer for everything. 'That remains an ongoing matter,' he replied when first asked to report progress. 'Our internal discussions have not come to a conclusion, but we hope to make a decision in March.' He continued to find excuses: 'It will be one of the next things I do' and 'In my considered view it would be wise to defer judgement.' He was a complete spin doctor of inactivity – a master at producing phrases that hid his laziness. By the end of the meeting he had produced even more: 'It's on my list'; 'I'm on to that one'; 'Following the correct procedure takes time'; 'I think it's wise to wait before making a move.'

In the time it takes to think up an excuse, most deeds could have been done. To avoid stress and increase efficiency: 'Do it now.'

Lists

Stressed executives can become obsessed by making lists and writing strategy papers, often late into the night, being keen to solve all their problems and start the next day with a clean sheet. Lists can help, but they need discipline. You only need two lists:

1. A big list of everything you need to do.
2. Your Top Five priorities.

Put your big list on an A4 pad and always keep it with you. You can put the list on an electronic device, but I feel safer with paper. Treat the list as a substitute for your memory. List everything. My approach is illustrated by the following story:

> I was just leaving the house early on a Monday morning when Alex shouted from upstairs, 'Can you bring back red polish for the children's shoes?' I played a 7.30 a.m. game of tennis before a busy day at the office. As well as the monthly board meeting, I recorded a training video, walked round the office for half and hour, made several phone calls, sent some handwritten notes to

shops that had had a good week and, on the way home, called to see an aunt who lives on her own.

The sales figures were good and I was keen to tell Alex about my productive day. I was taken aback by the first question as I walked through the door: 'Have you got the red polish?'

As far as Alex was concerned my successful day had been a complete failure. I had failed to put the polish on my list. I immediately wrote 'Red Polish' on my A4 pad which already had the following entries: NA floor, Gareth £300, Yates Wine, Helen chest waxing.

I had better explain how such a bizarre collection of items is relevant to running a chain of shoe repair shops:

- NA floor: shopfitters in Newton Abbot had left the floor behind our watch repair counter on a distinct slant.
- Gareth £300: Gareth, a shop manager, lives in a flat with no car parking. He wants a £300 company loan to purchase materials to create a hardcore area.
- Yates Wine: a few days ago when I was in Chester I noticed that Yates Wine Lodge had some displays worth copying.
- Helen chest waxing: Bob Northover, our manager in Taunton, was having his chest waxed to raise money for the NSPCC. As a local beauty parlour will be

doing the deed in four weeks' time, I need to tell Helen to put it in the newsletter.

I should do everything straight away, but even with a mobile phone you don't do everything immediately, so a notepad is my constant companion. At the end of each day I transfer scribbled notes onto my A4 pad. I tick every item as it is dealt with but I don't cross it out. Telling someone does not guarantee that action has been taken. Everything stays on the list until I am certain that the job has been done, and even then I don't throw the list away. Every three or four months I have a clear out. I go through all the old lists and create a new schedule of things remaining to be done and ideas that are still important. My list-making is an obsession, but it works. Despite my lousy memory, colleagues think I never forget.

The following day I achieved absolutely nothing, I flitted from one task to another, was interrupted by unproductive phone calls and spent 20 minutes looking for a piece of paper that was right in front of me. The day was saved by my A4 pad. Despite my apparent disorganisation I had done everything on the list. I even arrived home with a tin of red polish.

These lists help to avoid the stress caused by irritating detail, but the Top Five priority list does most good. When you are thinking straight, list the five most important things your business needs to do, and don't be tempted to change it.

Avoid major decisions when surrounded by anxiety. Businesses evolve, they don't benefit when a Chief Executive flounders from policy to policy.

An executive who is suffering a crisis of confidence keeps questioning everything about the business, thinking that things are about to go terribly wrong. If he is desperately looking for the big idea to put the company back on track, the priority list will help him to stick to the strategy.

It won't stop him worrying, but should help him to worry less about things that don't matter.

The Doomsday scenario

Here is a challenge for the downbeat business leader. Write the most pessimistic forecast you can imagine. This doomsday prediction is actually quite a sophisticated form of risk assessment and will probably not seem to be as bad as you expected in your darkest moments. Far from making you feel more depressed, it will encourage you to look on the flip side. Before long you will be able to reverse the situation, and write the dream scenario that will help you to return to a world of positive thinking.

Do the nice bits

It is a big mistake to think you are good at everything. As Chief Executive you must take responsibility for strategy and communication, but you don't have to be an expert in finance, property, personnel or marketing. Let your team deal with the detail and only get involved in the bits you know and enjoy. You don't have to spend your time making tough choices, just concentrate on the easy decisions. If in doubt, do nothing. Don't think that indecision is a sign of weakness. Doing nothing is very often the right thing to do.

Companies thrive on consistency, and colleagues need leadership, but they don't like regular changes in direction as new strategies often make matters worse. Good leaders resist the temptation to keep making decisions and have the courage to do nothing. A lot of businesses suffer from over-management and boardroom interference. If you simply stick to the things you enjoy and do well and make the easy decisions that you know are right, your colleagues will follow your leadership with confidence.

Try to keep busy

For 20 years I have kept my old diaries. They are full of activity but occasionally there is a blank month where hardly anything happened. Those diaries show that stress can keep you hidden in the office, unwilling to meet people or risk unfamiliar situations. Whenever an invitation arrives you search for a reason to turn it down; travel plans are cut because you are too busy at the office. You need to be brave: don't go into your shell and mope, and don't duck every invitation. You must get out and do something. In my worse moments Alex has always sent me out to visit our shops: 'That's what you're good at,' she says.

The best cure for stress is success. A personal achievement, however small, will help to build confidence. You won't achieve anything sitting in your office – even a tortoise doesn't make progress unless he sticks his neck out! It's difficult to face the world when that's the last thing you want to do. Against your better judgement, keep a full diary and create the chance to prove that you are still successful.

Beware of minor mistakes

Anxiety is usually caused by overwork and the pressure of major problems, but it is often a minor incident that turns worry into stress. Forgetting an appointment, filling a diesel car with unleaded, calling a close friend by the wrong name, losing a credit card or cruel remarks from a colleague are things that will never threaten the future of your business but can be the catalyst that triggers off stress and depression.

Most little mistakes are forgotten in minutes, but suddenly you do something silly that you think about for days. Why did I do that? If only I had been more careful. What else have I been doing wrong? The little mistake keeps turning itself round in your mind and becomes a big problem.

I have learned a lot from golf. One of the most humbling parts of the game is the fact that when you are playing badly and you think the world is watching, no one else cares. The same applies to your minor blunders – no one else cares, so why should you?

Time to delegate

A period of depression is a good time to delegate. Don't interfere, let your people get on with their jobs. They'll do much better without you. You may be worried that by standing back you are not doing your job – not true. Even if some of your team are at the top of your worry list, keep clear; your constant anxious interference will be irritating. They will come to you if they really need help. In the meantime, practise 'Upside Down Management'.

* * * * *

Writing this chapter has been more difficult than I expected. It's not because I'm bothered about revealing a more personal side of my business life. I'm very happy to talk about stress if that helps others with the same problem. The difficult bit is to recall how stress affected me. You remember the good times, the painful experiences are hidden in the back of your memory – which is good news as the future has never matched up to any of my moods of deep despondency. Sometimes it's hard to believe that stress will disappear, but as soon as you return to top form, life is wonderful. Once again you realise that there is nothing much to worry about.

Chapter Eight

LET YOUR CONSCIENCE BE YOUR GUIDE

If government practised Upside Down Management (not that it is a political possibility) they would be amazed what could be achieved without all the business rules and regulations. Most companies have highly moral motives. Red tape is written to trap dishonest traders and uncaring employers; the law usually misses its target and instead of trapping the bad guy creates unnecessary work for the vast majority of businesses that do have a social conscience. But we in business only have ourselves to blame. Commercial reputation for fair play is tarnished by shareholders who want instant results and executives who flit to a new job every three years, developing their CV at their company's expense.

Too many managers think that you always have to be tough, unbending and super selfish. Compassion is seen as a sign of weakness (unless you are bidding at a charity auction or ticking the Corporate Social Responsibility box). I have news for them – the best entrepreneurs have great flair *and* a sensitive conscience.

Bad business

The average tenure of a football manager is less than three years (and you can understand why) but even in football short-term appointments do more harm than good. I reluctantly admit – as a Manchester City supporter! – that Manchester United and Arsenal have shown that consistent leadership brings better results.

Professional managers brought in to rescue a failing business often follow a predictable pattern. The new broom tours the company to meet the people (for most employees this will be the only time they see him). Following the tour he produces a frank report and announces a cost-cutting campaign. The first financial statement is accompanied by a profit warning but the shares go up because the profit fall is due to exceptional items that give the new executive elbow room to work his miracle in the months ahead. A significant number of the front line employees are made redundant, before our new Chief Executive launches his master plan and new people arrive, especially in the management suite. Sometimes the plan works but often it doesn't and within two years the Chief Executive will resign ahead of a new profits warning. Revolving doors in the boardroom do not help a business. Every company needs a long-term leader with flair and a conscience.

Having been a buyer, I can criticise the bullying tactics used by big business buyers against defenceless suppliers. In 1979 I spent the summer developing a new fashion shoe range for the following spring. Styles found in Italy were copied by a manufacturer based in Bacup, Lancashire. The range looked good, so I placed large orders. I was taking a substantial risk, but as soon as the first shoes were put on sale I knew I was on a winner.

When the British Shoe Corporation chief buyer visited the factory, he was amazed to see how much of the production was going to Timpson and that we were getting deliveries nearly a month before BSC (I placed my orders two months before they did). The factory was given an ultimatum: 'Don't deliver Timpson another pair until all our orders have arrived in our warehouse, otherwise you'll never get another order from us.' This was a totally unacceptable way of using buying power. BSC had 25% of the market, I had 4%, and the only way I could compete was by being quicker and smarter, but my advantage was being snubbed out by blackmail. The manufacturer told me the story because he knew me so well; other people wouldn't have had the courage. I wrote a letter to the BSC buyer asking him to confirm whether the story was true, and quickly got a reply: 'I can assure you there is no truth in rumours you describe in your letter.' I got my shoes on time and we had an excellent season.

In recent years, plenty of bully-boy tactics have been used by big retailers. Several companies have asked suppliers for an extra contribution to their marketing budget 'to help to combat tough trading'. A popular tactic is to take extra credit (60 days instead of the 28 days in the contract); if you resist the request you can expect to be delisted, because 'everyone else has agreed to our request'. This is cheating. I am not a soft touch but I do have a conscience and as far as I am concerned a deal is a deal. These draconian tactics are short-term measures that often backfire. Suppliers get their own back by increasing next year's price and giving preferential treatment to their more honourable customers.

A friend who came to stay told me his problem as we walked round the garden, 'What's got into you, Doug?' I asked. 'Where do I start?' he replied. 'It began as the deal of a life-time, the chance to open several stores at once. At first Susan, the brand manager, and her boss, Mark, were very positive. They asked for proposals to put before Tuesday's Divisional board. I worked through the weekend and sent an e-mail on Monday morning. I heard nothing so I rang a few times and got voice mail. On Thursday I tried an e-mail; "we will respond on Monday" was the reply. On Wednesday they proposed a conference call for the following morning, and at last I could agree heads of terms.

I cancelled all engagements and waited for the call, but their mood had changed. Mark was sarcastic and off-hand: "Your offer is way off the mark," he sneered, "you are living in fantasy land wasting our time. I need a £50,000 monthly guarantee in writing for our senior management meeting next week." We met his deadline with a revised proposal providing everything he wanted. On Thursday morning I rang to check that our offer had arrived. "Mark has gone away for the weekend," said his PA. I rang again at midday on Monday. "I've got your offer," said Mark, "but I haven't had time to read it."

A week went by without a word and I rang Susan who sounded irritated. I felt slightly guilty that I was pestering her. "The deal must be signed off by my Divisional Director," she said. "I can't see her until tomorrow." I heard nothing for three weeks then Susan rang. "Mark has decided to completely change the deal," she said tersely. "We are close to signing with one of your competitors; to be considered you must submit a better offer by 8.30 a.m. tomorrow.'"

His story made me think. I posed myself a question: What is ethical trading? I'm not just talking about fair trade in Third World countries – I include honesty and courtesy towards customers, colleagues, suppliers and even competitors.

I want to deal with people I trust and I want to win their respect by keeping to the moral high ground. With this in mind I wrote some guidelines for my colleagues to follow:

The Timpson Code of Ethical Trading

Timpson will discriminate in favour of companies who deal with decency and good manners.

Equal authority – We expect executives to have the authority to make quick decisions without reference to committees or senior management.

Easy to contact – During a deal we expect everyone to answer phone calls, give an immediate response to voice mail or e-mails, no one to hide in a meeting and no one to take holidays without telling us.

Total honesty – The truth and nothing but the truth, we don't like lies big or small; even little fibs are irritating, such as: 'no one told me you called' or 'I was in a meeting'.

Be polite – Whoever you are, be pleasant. There is no excuse for sarcasm, talking down, being arrogant or failing to say thank you.

A deal is a deal – We don't trust people who change their minds and we don't like dealing with bullies, for example:

> *Dear supplier Due to difficult trading times we need your support so have decided to take an extra 28 days' credit.*

Companies talk about fair deals and ethical trading when they are far from fair and certainly not ethical. Should we blame *Dragons' Den* and *The Apprentice*, or is there a special MBA course in abuse and bad manners? Bullying, arrogance and dishonesty might create a macho image and win a few deals, but the person getting rolled over will never forget, and, given the chance, they will get revenge. Managers of today should remember that in the end the good guy usually wins.

I get really angry when, as a customer, I experience the thick end of selfish arrogance and management incompetence. The cause of my irritation is nearly always a big business. Too many organisations make stupid and basic mistakes:

1.   They make rules for their customers to follow.
2.   They think their computers are always right.
3.   They take weeks to reply to letters.
4.   They are always in a meeting and hide behind their back office team.
5.   If you telephone, no one answers, or you talk to a machine. (Why can 118118 answer within two rings while other call centres take up to 20 minutes?)
6.   They make it difficult to complain.

Some of these chief executives have lost contact with their customers; they live in a world of management speak, KPIs, government guidelines and best practice. They spend plenty of time with analysts and do their bit to save the world – but none of these things is as important as looking after customers. I suspect few big companies would agree with me that the way to satisfy a justified complaint is to offer the customer more compensation than they ever expected.

Despite my criticism, business is better at customer service than Whitehall. I have sent several letters to Ministers and Government Departments, but have never received even an acknowledgement within four weeks and half of the time I got no response at all – they simply do not realise that the public are their customers. No one should think they are more important than the people who ultimately pay their wages.

Look after your superstars

In recent years corporate social responsibility seems to have become a big box well worth ticking. It won't be long before the *Sunday Times* is producing a list of the most socially responsible companies, including a table based on everyone's carbon footprint. Perhaps a government department will produce an official audit led by a regulator of good practice using a social responsibility rating. We are losing the plot. Thankfully I own our business and can be guided by my own conscience not public opinion, media hype or government guidelines.

It may sound like a cliché, but it's true that charity begins at home. The number one cause I support is the team of colleagues who work for our company. When I was a child I wondered why my father often referred to employees as if they were members of the family – now I know. My priority is the business and the people who work in it. I must look after our colleagues and our customers *before* doing my bit to help the outside world.

Dealing with drongos

We are responsible for the code of conduct inside our business. We try to create a community in which colleagues care for each other. Any form of discrimination or bullying in the workplace is regarded as gross misconduct. We think it is important to produce a great place to work – and you can only do that if colleagues work well together, respect each other and give every new recruit a warm welcome.

Despite a reputation as a caring boss, I am not a benevolent soft touch. You can't be nice to everyone. You can't be a good boss unless you say goodbye to the drongos. Poor performers do a lot of damage to a business. They undermine morale and annoy your superstars, costing a lot of money in the process. It is irritating to pay compensation, but paying a financial fare-well to a drongo is always money well spent. Avoid wasting time on difficult people. Managers spend a lot of their working week with people who are useless, doing disciplinary hear-ings, retraining and counselling. Abandon the lost causes and spend your time with the people who can make you more money. One of the best ways to look after your people is to make sure they are working alongside talented colleagues.

On the other hand, I am also wary of prima donnas – pompous big-headed loudmouths are as irritating to the rest of your team as they are to you, so don't be intimidated by claims that they are indispensable. No one is. Dispense with their services as soon as possible.

Sadly, from time to time, you will make a mistake and promote someone to a job too far. Step in straight away and move that person to a role more suited to his or her talents. Remember that you are to blame if some people are given the wrong job. Don't come up with a compromise; fudging doesn't work. If someone is promoted beyond his ability, put him back into his old job and be generous in compensation. Don't set him another impossible task or send him down a blind alley. If you hide an incompetent person by giving him a dead-end job, you will live to regret it.

These are tough decisions, but you must be cruel to be kind to the rest of the business. The better the quality of your team, the better they will work together.

Plenty of praise

I have covered the tough part of the job, so now for something much more pleasant.

Too much management time can be spent with the poor performers. Make a conscious effort to spend more of your working week with the superstars – and praise them 10 times as much as you criticise. Praise is a brilliant management tool, it builds morale and is a great motivator, but many managers are reluctant to hand out compliments. Here are some of my favourite ways to say 'well done':

Friday phone call – Our trading week ends on a Thursday and the first indication I get of our performance is gathered by the area teams who ring up every shop and then Timpson House. Some years ago our IT team wanted to write a computer program that would electronically contact our shop tills overnight and gather the information on the Area Manager's behalf. I wouldn't let them do it. When they contact their shops our Area Managers don't just discuss business. As well as talking about trading and saying 'well done', they can ask 'How was the holiday?', 'Is your wife recovering from her operation?' 'How did your son do in the football match?' Those conversations are much more valuable than a cost-saving computer system.

Simple ways to say 'well done' – It is well worth going to the trouble of saying 'well done' in a tangible way. A bottle of wine or a box of chocolates (making sure you know what they like); Saturday off to watch the football, plus the tickets; a meal out or a pop concert. Upside Down Management allows our managers to praise people in any way that they feel is appropriate.

Money – £10 notes in a surprise envelope are always welcome, but make sure you pay the tax as well – you don't want your deserving colleagues to get a shock when they get their next pay packets.

Scratch card – Here's an idea we borrowed from Asda. Every week find some people who have done well and give them a company-created scratch card. They scratch the foil to reveal their own prize, which could be a £5 note, a meal out, two days off, a bottle of wine or a weekend break.

Public praise – Let everyone see how well your colleague has done by putting the good deed in the next newsletter or, even better, try to get your colleague's picture and story in the local press.

Award ceremonies – Every evening out is an excuse for an award ceremony. Whatever the celebration, every company event can include a few trophies, which prize winners will keep as a treasured memento of a special occasion.

Holidays – Major success deserves special recognition. If you are amazed by a colleague's performance, why not give him or her an extra week off and pay for the air fare to the person's favourite destination.

Holiday homes – One of the most popular perks we provide to colleagues is free accommodation at one of our holiday homes. We have an apartment in Spain and holiday chalets in Bournemouth and Blackpool. In 2010 we are opening another two, with a further four apartments planned for 2011. The idea came from Richer Sounds, who sold us the apartment in Spain. We have a long waiting list – that's why we are expanding our portfolio (a sound property investment). But even if we have enough space to satisfy demand, we don't let holiday homes to drongos!! The accommodation is totally free; all our colleagues have to pay for is travel, food and drink. A free holiday is a great way to reward loyal colleagues, which also involves the rest of their family.

Handwritten notes – The handwritten letter sent to a colleague's home is still my favourite form of praise, especially if you enclose a significant cheque inside the envelope, which has also been written using the same fountain pen and is sent using a first-class stamp.

Praise is just one part of being a caring manager. Here are some other things that good managers can do to help their colleagues:

Promises – Never make promises you can't keep. It doesn't matter what it is: 'I'll get you a new shirt', 'I'll send a new key-cutting machine' or 'I'll give you a loan'. When you make a promise you must keep it. Good management depends on trust. If you don't do what you promise, you lose respect. Never break a promise.

Listen – Mediocre managers do a lot of talking and too little listening. If you want to gain respect and be a great boss, listen carefully to what your colleagues have to say. You can do a lot of good simply by listening to someone who has a problem, and you can improve the business by listening to those colleagues who have new ideas.

Be their friend – It is not weak management to be a friend as well as a boss. After all, as my father taught me, your colleagues are part of the family, but there is no need to let your friendship spill over into your social life.

Provide sympathy – If a colleague loses a member of her family, she may well turn to you for help. The sympathetic letter and attendance at the funeral makes a big difference. This is another time when you need to be a good listener.

Time off for the dentist – If someone has a problem, don't look at the rule book, use common sense. If one of your people has toothache, let him go to the dentist; if he's in pain, there is not much point in keeping him at work. And don't even think of asking him to make up the time at a later date.

Lend money – There are times when £10 or £20 can make all the difference. If you've got a budding superstar who is stuck for cash, don't bother with all the official paper work or apply to the hardship fund, just lend her the money. If she is a colleague you can trust, you'll get the money back; if you don't, you'll suddenly have learned a lot more about her character.

Family matters – The better you know your colleagues the better boss you will be. It isn't just a question of knowing about them – the more you know about their family the better, and you will then be able to relate to their personality. If a colleague's mother is ill, he may need time off work, or if one of his children is a budding athlete, let him go to the regional finals. Help your colleagues to fulfil their lives at home and they will do a much better job while they are at work.

Wedding anniversaries – It is easy in our business to remember everyone's birthday because they get the day off and a month before the birthday People Support send you a reminder to make sure you send a card. But really knowing your people means going a stage further. If you've got a note of their wedding anniversary, send a card and pay for a night out. It shows your colleague's partner how much you care.

Visit the sick – When illness interferes with work it is a boss's job to keep in touch and, if possible, pay a visit. Sometimes the threat of the boss calling can stop people taking 'sickies', but mostly it simply shows how much you care about your team.

Timpson Culture Committee

Looking after your people is right at the centre of good business. You can't do enough to amaze the top performers. Sincere care doesn't follow a set of rules, it is instinctive and often occurs on the spur of the moment. We are proud to have a culture based on trust with lots of ways to look after loyal colleagues: our hardship fund, holiday homes, the bonus scheme, birthdays off and many more. Collectively I call these things our Magic Dust – the special bits we do that create the Timpson character. But I am always concerned about how long that culture can survive. I fear that we may forget how we created our success and allow the things that really matter to lapse.

To keep the Magic Dust on our agenda we formed the Timpson Culture Committee, consisting of seven people who monitor the vital elements of our management style and promote new ways to make the company even better. Each member keeps a close eye on some aspect of our culture: the benefits, such as football tickets; the truth behind our management style; and the openness of our communication. They meet with James and me twice a year to make sure we are still spreading the Magic Dust.

The Culture Committee makes sure that we still keep important values close to the heart of the business. We continue to trust everyone, even though we watch them carefully; we pamper the great employees, look after the loyal people, and support the mavericks. We want everyone to act as if they were part of the family. We provide advice when needed, care for colleagues in difficulty, and while creating success we also have fun.

Giving more back

Our colleagues come first. They take priority over corporate social responsibility, and when it comes to charity only one person is going to tell me how to be generous. The source of my altruistic advice comes from an expert very close to home ... Alex.

Fostering

My wife, Alex, brought something extra into our marriage. On the way back from taking our son, Edward, to nursery school, Alex was stopped for speeding. The policeman, filling out his form, asked: 'Do you have a job or are you a housewife?' To which Alex crossly replied, 'I have two jobs, I am a housewife and a mother.'

Alex was a nursery nurse (a nanny) when I first met her. From leaving school at 16, until she married at the age of 21, her life was spent looking after children. The gap from childcare was short lived. Thirteen months after we married, Victoria was born. James arrived two years later and Edward two years after that. We were set for a typical family life.

I had a new, stimulating job and we had moved into the house that Alex regarded as the perfect family home.

It all changed when our youngest child, Edward, went to school. Perhaps it was the policeman who queried Alex's employment who started the whole thing off. Whatever the reason, Alex very quickly found long days with no children in the house difficult to take. She tried charity committees, but soon discovered that she was a lady who did not lunch. In addition to being a housewife, she needed another job.

One day, she spotted an advertisement for foster carers, and that was it. Once Alex has an idea, she goes for it. Soon I was being interviewed by my first social worker. Morven Sowerbutts met us to find out whether we knew anything about fostering (which I didn't) and see if we were really determined to go ahead (which Alex, of course, was).

A more serious, in-depth interview followed. Two of our friends were interrogated and another social worker checked that Morven had the right impression. Eventually, we were approved by the fostering panel as short-term foster parents, but nothing happened for six months.

Fostering had gone from my mind when, one Friday, I returned from work to find two extra children. The boys, aged 3 and 4, were free-range, not used to regular bed or meal times, and had never used a knife, fork or spoon. Their

language impressed our children. The 3-year-old rode a tri-
cycle round the room shouting 'f*** off' at the top of his
voice, and they quickly copied him!

Their behaviour was different, as I discovered the following
morning when I took the two boys shopping to Wilmslow.
In Silvios, the baker's shop on Grove Street, the 4-year-old
tugged fiercely on my arm. 'John, John that woman's got big
busters.' Everyone looked at me. I smiled at the well-endowed
lady, with an expression which I hope said: 'Very sorry, I'm
a new foster parent and this is my first day.' But the children
soon fell into our routine, and after three weeks they were
part of the family.

On the fostering front, Alex did the work, and I got the nice
bits. As the weeks turned to months, more of the nice bits
appeared. I told bedtime stories and took them for walks in
the woods, while Alex helped them to develop as people.
It was amazing to see them grow up in such a short time.
They came with little knowledge and had never seen a cow
or a sheep. When they looked outside our window on the
first morning they asked to play in the park (our garden).
When we went to north Wales, they called the sea a 'big
puddle'.

Fostering changed our approach to dinner parties, which, in
any case, I find conversationally difficult. Then we started
fostering. It is a subject you cannot avoid. Someone asks you

about your family and that starts it off. 'How many children do you have?' It's a simple question for most people, but was quite difficult for me. I would reply 'Well, it depends on what you mean.' Immediately my inquisitor would think that I had a string of ex-wives. To clear the air I would say that we are foster parents. Fostering would then dominate the conversation and there would be expressions of sympathy, disbelief and embarrassed admiration.

* A question that people always ask is: *'Don't you feel awful when they leave?'*

We were approved as short-term foster parents, and this meant a maximum of six months. The first foster children arrived in May. We were not asked to any case conferences to plan the boys' future – indeed no future had been planned. The boys left three weeks before Christmas and went straight to a children's home in nearby Knutsford. As soon as they had gone it was clear that Alex had become emotionally attached. She waited until New Year but could wait no longer and went to the Children's Home, peered through the fence, and saw the two boys in the playground. That visit was repeated several times during the next four months until Alex heard that the boys had moved to another foster home. She had learned a difficult lesson and never got so emotionally attached to any of the 90 children who followed.

- Another favourite dinner party question is: '*Which children do you remember most?*'

Families of three stick in the memory; they changed our routine by sheer weight of numbers. Once I arrived from a day trip to London to find an extra three pairs of school shoes and three pairs of trainers in the kitchen that Alex had put out for me to clean. That family (a girl and her two young brothers) argued incessantly, from 5.30 a.m. until bedtime. It took all of Alex's experience to cope with them. By the time she had achieved harmony among the foster children, the rest of us were so tired that we started arguing among ourselves.

Our most disruptive visitors were 6-month-old triplets. They only stayed for four weeks but we will never forget them. Alex had extra help from the Social Services during the day, and I was on duty at night. Early morning and late night feeding were a joint effort. We started at 5.30 a.m. to ensure that the triplets were fed before our own children went to school and I left for work. Alex relished the task and enjoyed taking the triplets out in a specially made three-berth buggy to incredulous stares from Wilmslow shoppers. Strangers approached Alex with an odd question: '*Are these real live triplets?*'

Short-term fostering is no longer just for six months. Two boys who stayed with us for the best part of a year became

very much part of the family. We went to their school con-
certs, a nativity play, parent/teacher meetings, and their
school friends came to play at our home. We got to know
their parents well. They were addicted to drugs and were in
a rehabilitation centre 50 miles away. Over the months, Alex
made several trips with the children to see their parents. The
marriage eventually broke down and the children went back
to live with their mother.

When the calls came from Social Services we had no idea
how long the children were going to stay. One enquiry came
just before we were going on holiday. We had booked a
family fortnight in a house in Portugal and Social Services
rang five days before we were due to depart. It was late July,
and no other suitable foster parents were available. The only
answer was for the two boys to join our family party, but
that proved to be more difficult than expected. The holiday
company were less than sympathetic; they wanted to charge
a premium rate for the late booking. I ignored them and
arranged separate flights through a bucket shop. Six months
later, they were still with us. The older boy became our only
long-term foster child and stayed for 10 years.

Alex even managed to increase the size of her family shortly
after a hysterectomy! During convalescence Alex started
talking about adoption and one of our Social Workers listened. Early that summer Alex went back to the same chil-

dren's home in Knutsford where she had waved goodbye to our first foster children. I joined her on the second visit and for the first time met Roy, an undersized 6 year old, full of energy and a bag of nerves. After several visits, Roy came to live with us and shortly after his seventh birthday was adopted and became Oliver Timpson.

Alex felt she was in need of a real challenge and in Oliver she found one. In those days there was no help in preparation for adoption – we had never heard about 'attachment' problems. No one gave us the slightest hint that we were about to be put through a supreme test of parenting. Many children misbehave, they are disobedient and tell lies, but with Oliver this had become a way of life. Alex was undeterred. Oliver made progress but it was two steps forward and one step back. Schooling was difficult. Just when we thought he was settled, something went wrong and we moved him elsewhere. He had a beautiful treble voice and we persuaded him to join the Chester Cathedral choir. All was going well until he fell out with the choir master (something to do with passing around sexy playing cards during evensong).

Oliver has retained the most endearing personality. It's that charm that makes him even more frustrating. For over 27 years we have experienced considerable despair and relief. We learned a lot, but the greatest feeling is frustration.

When Oliver was 13 we adopted Henry, who was two weeks old when he arrived as a foster child. At a time when most people are thinking of grandchildren, Henry became our fifth child.

- Another dinner party question is: *'What do your own children think of it all?'*

Edward showed that it was not all plain sailing when the first child arrived; he hid in his room. But later he took such an interest in fostering that (at the age of 16) he lectured the whole of Uppingham School about fostering and adoption. Later he became a barrister, specialising in family law. In 2008 he was elected MP for Crewe and Nantwich and quickly became a member of the select committee for Children, Schools and Families.

Our daughter, Victoria, developed a career as a primary school teacher and James, Timpson's current Managing Director, inherited his mother's social conscience too.

- Another popular dinner party question is: *'How do you get on with the Social Workers?'*

In most respects, we got on very well. The Social Services has steadily improved, but in one way things deteriorated. Every time the government tried to improve childcare services, or legislated to prevent an abuse recurring, they created more paper work. Our social workers called it 'pressure of work' and 'lack of resources'. It now takes far too long to resolve the future plans for children in care. Sometimes the social workers take so long to make up their minds that it is too late. As one of our social workers said, 'My computer has moved to the middle of my desk.'

One mother of four children who briefly came into our care, rang Alex out of the blue two years later. She had taken an overdose and wanted Alex to look after her children. Alex took her to hospital and contacted the social workers. That was the first of several such emergency calls. On each subsequent occasion, Alex brought the children back to our house and the problem disappeared.

One mother wrote to Alex to say that she was expecting another child and wanted her son to stay with us when she gave birth. I had forgotten about the letter when Alex woke me at 2.00 a.m.; the mother was in labour and asked us to collect her son. I arrived back at 3.00 a.m. not only with the boy but also with his very smelly guinea pig.

Alex helps parents as well as children. At times our telephone has become a helpline with Alex becoming the agony aunt on childcare. Problems at school, difficult teenagers, 'what do I do with my new baby?' and, several times, 'I don't think I can cope with our adopted child'. When our telephone rings, I know it's for Alex. The clients of her helpline don't realise that there are times when Alex also has problems she needs to discuss – we too need time to talk.

Whenever you think Alex has met every possible challenge, she finds another one.

In the early 1990s, we went to Romania. Alex decided that two small Romanian children were just what we required to complete our family. We visited four children's homes and stayed with a delightful family who had connections in Cheshire. We met a Romanian lawyer who explained the difficulties of Romanian law – and he was right. For once Alex was unsuccessful. We found Romania fascinating and went back to a family wedding at the house in which we had stayed. Edward, who had joined us on that trip, regards it as one of the most memorable moments of his life.

- As the dinner party draws to a close, there is still one more question. '*What are your most vivid memories?*'

I remember the big groups for Sunday lunch – often a dozen or more sitting round the table. Particularly the awkward 11 year old who ran away and hid in our large garden just as we were about to drive to the airport to go on a skiing holiday. I remember going to Euro Disney, with Alex leading a group with a mother and her children all on their first trip abroad.

Once when we had three short-term foster children staying with us I went to the local garage to buy newspapers and sweets before breakfast. The woman behind the counter gave a sympathetic smile. She asked about the children and I explained that they were fostered. 'I've always thought of doing that,' she said. I have heard this remark many times. Lots of people think about fostering but few do anything about it. Thanks to Alex we did.

I am lucky. Alex brought experiences into our lives that few people will have had the privilege to enjoy, and her attitude has had a major influence on our business. Alex has incredible energy and drive, which is almost entirely directed towards helping other people. In the process she provides a moral compass with a strong magnetic force which has helped to direct our business – not just to tick the social responsibility box but also to satisfy our conscience. Most of my life I have lived with a prime exponent of unselfish generosity. The business has learned a lot from her example.

In 2006 Alex received the MBE for services to children and declared that she would like to foster one last sibling group (which brought the total number of children up to 90). This short-term placement extended to two years. They were what Social Services called a challenging family. When they arrived they were aged 5, 3 and 2. It was in many ways one of the most successful placements we had, and we really felt we had made a difference. They also confirmed our suspicion that it was time to retire as foster carers, and we de-registered in 2009.

Alex still looks after children. Our eight grandchildren get plenty of her time, but she still keeps regular contact with many of our former foster families. She has also found a new role as a Home Start volunteer, spending several hours a week helping a family to develop their parenting skills.

While all this has been going on Alex has been my key adviser and more recently masterminded the fantastic success of The White Eagle at Rhoscolyn on Anglesey, the pub we bought near our holiday home because 'Alex wanted somewhere decent to eat'.

Our approach to charity

The NSPCC/*ChildLine*

Alex and the fostering experience has had a major influence on the Timpson approach to charity. Early in 1999 Alex and I were invited by the NSPCC to a dinner. I knew that I would eventually have to pay for the free meal, but Alex liked the idea of dinner with the Duke of Westminster in his dining room at Eaton Hall. 'You will just have to put a few pounds in the raffle,' she said. But there wasn't a raffle. I never touched my wallet all evening. On the way home Alex was enthused: 'That was great, you must do something special to thank them.' I was awake until 3.00 a.m. worrying about what to do. I told Alex my solution as I poured the early morning tea: 'Bits of glue and lots of holes,' I said. 'What on earth are you talking about?' said Alex wearily. 'Well, we do lots of jobs for free like gluing soles and putting holes in belts,' I said; 'if we ask these customers to give some money to the NSPCC it should bring in £500 a week. We could make a video to encourage employees to support the fund-raising, we could organise sponsored walks, run in the London marathon.'

'You're all talk,' interrupted Alex, 'it will be forgotten before you even get to the office. All you think about is shoes, keys and bloody watch repairs.'

Eight weeks later we showed the video to our area managers and collected £200 within 10 minutes. I shouldn't have worried about whether street-wise shoe repairers would respond to a charity appeal. In the first week our shops collected £3,000. Within a month they were running their own fund-raising events. Alan in Stafford sat outside his shop on a Saturday, had all his hair shaved off, and collected £400. Bob in Taunton had his chest waxed and raised £3,000 (£1 per hair!).

In 20 months we raised £240,000 – it wasn't just the NSPCC treasurer who was pleased. Customers liked the idea, Alex was happy, and I enjoyed record profits. Most of all, our colleagues were proud of being part of a company with a conscience.

Two years later I asked our area managers whether they wanted to continue fundraising, and the response was unanimous. They changed from the NSPCC to ChildLine, which has been our company's charity ever since. For several years I joined Esther Rantzen as a Trustee of ChildLine until it merged with the NSPCC.

Fundraising is an important part of Timpson life. Our newsletter features Captain Cash (alias my son James) who gives significant sums to good causes every month. Recently Captain Cash bought a football team strip, funded a special needs teacher at a local school and made a contribution towards the building of a local community hall. Some colleagues want to raise money for their own particular charity, that is why you won't find a ChildLine box in some of our shops – they do the free jobs for the cause that is particularly close to their heart. Since we started raising money in 1999 – mainly through our free jobs scheme – we have raised over £2 million and continue to collect about £6,000 every week.

After Adoption

Our strong connection with ChildLine brought another unexpected advantage. Whenever charitable requests came to my office, I could politely reply that we only support our company charity. Apart from modest donations to friends who go trekking, cycling or run marathons for their pet charity, I kept to ChildLine and ignored approaches from everywhere else. Then one took my eye.

The letter was from After Adoption based in Manchester. I met their chief executive, Lynn Charlton, who explained what it was all about. After Adoption help people involved in the adoption process – children, adoptive parents and the birth parents whose children have been taken away. After Adoption have a family finding service but most of their time is spent providing counselling and advice.

Alex and I took a close interest in their 'Safe Base' project – a support programme to help adoptive parents to deal with the difficulties that often occur with adopted children. We talked to the team and some parents before observing a few counselling sessions. Being an adoptive parent isn't easy; sometimes children's ability to bond and trust is so damaged by previous experiences that they can't respond to the most loving parents and do everything they can to resist a strong relationship. This lack of trust leads the children to regularly test out their adoptive parents and attempt to prove, what they believe deep down, that they are unlovable. A child will often appear like an angel to an outsider while causing chaos within the family, and the parents will not only have to cope with a troubled child but also with critical friends who feel that the child needs rescuing from these angry up-tight parents.

For years, children and adults have both been the victims of ignorance. Little was known of 'attachment' and the major problems it can cause for children, teenagers and adults. Alex learned about Attachment Disorder at a course run by our local Social Services. Dan Hughes, an unsung genius, spoke to a small group of foster carers and explained the missing link. Lack of attachment during the first years of life can make a child stressed, unhappy and angry and often leads to bad behaviour.

A baby totally relies on help – normally from parents. Parents usually help their children to develop an emotional attachment, and the first two years are the most important. With the help of responsive carers. children can grow up feeling good about themselves – as valued members of society. But it doesn't always work out like that. Instead of getting care and attention, some children are badly treated – causing attachment problems. As a result, the children feel anxious and unwanted, unlovable and unworthy of attention – they feel rejected, stressed, unhappy and angry, and could show these feelings through poor behaviour.

The commitment of foster carers and adoptive parents will be severely tested, and the lack of confidence and respect will be a handicap for years to come. As a result children can grow up with no real sense of self – they lack confidence, may not trust others, are prone to impulsive action and lack responsibility.

Alex and I know how these adoptive parents feel as we experienced the whole range of emotions with Oliver. Life with Ollie has been a roller coaster ride – it would have been much easier if we had had the help of After Adoption's 'Safe Base' and understood about 'Attachment'.

While discussing how the 'Safe Base' project could be developed, Lynn Charlton suggested that it could make a significant difference if more people knew about 'Attachment' and the effect it had on people's lives. We therefore decided to target those who had most to do with children: teachers, social workers, probation officers and doctors. As a result, I wrote one of my little Mr Men books, but instead of talking about management, this book simply explains the problems of 'Attachment' in a way that After Adoption could use to spread the message.

I am delighted to say that my little book seems to have filled a major gap and is now being distributed beyond After Adoption. It is helping to spread the 'Attachment' message to many groups connected with children in care throughout the UK. I've had great pleasure and satisfaction from working with After Adoption, who will receive all the royalties from this book.

Delamere Primary School

Many of our foster children went to our local school – Delamere Primary – and a few years ago Alex became a governor. In 2006 the school was threatened with closure – a review of Cheshire schools considered that Delamere was too small to be viable and the case was strengthened by a mediocre OFSTED inspection.

Alex leaned on me to become involved. We encouraged parents to write to councillors and I made a personal plea to the Director of Children's Services for Cheshire. I argued that we need small schools – the children we cared for thrived at Delamere, and they would have been swallowed up in a bigger school. To demonstrate my commitment we offered to inject £150,000 over five years to add to the school's curriculum and broaden the children's experience (modest compared with other entrepreneurs who had set up academies, but still important). I encouraged them to establish Delamere Primary as a centre of excellence – an example for other small schools to follow.

The closure plans were put on hold and, when the Chairman of the Governors moved to a job 100 miles away, Alex put my name forward as his successor. I was staggered by the amount of form filling and administration involved: the school had over 50 policy statements, lots of KPIs, an improvement plan and a five-year strategy statement.

Delamere, with only 43 pupils, had to complete the same forms as other schools that taught nearly 1,000. Over half of the Headteacher's week was taken up with paperwork.

Our extra cash helped, but the school also benefited from a bit of upside down management. I met some of the central administrators and persuaded them to let Steve Docking, the Headteacher, spend most of his time running the school. Steve spent our money wisely. He didn't invest in building, he introduced extra activities to enrich the lives of the children. The outside tuition he brought to the school included extra art, music, theatre, cooking and nature studies in nearby Delamere Forest. There has, since then, been a vast range of extra activities: canoeing, camping, orienteering and a visit to London, which included Westminster and *The Lion King*.

I asked Steve and his deputy, Julie, what had made the difference. 'It's the range of activities,' Julie replied, 'children now arrive in the morning and say, "What are we doing today?" Average children are over-performing and only this week, a new boy's mother told me it was the best week of school he has ever had. We probably aren't ticking as many boxes but we are certainly doing a much better job for the parents and children.' Within two years the school received an outstanding OFSTED report and pupil numbers had risen by nearly 50%. The school is no longer on the closure list.

Ex-Offenders

Many family businesses, to their credit, establish a family charitable trust to distribute funds to local and national charities. We don't have one; we prefer to concentrate on projects where we can become closely involved. In 2004 we realised that we were uniquely placed to help ex-offenders to get back into the world of work. The idea started when James visited a prison near Warrington. Matthew, the prisoner who showed James round, kept to his script but couldn't hide his sparky personality. 'Ring when you get out and I'll find you a job,' said James. For the next six months Matthew worked for us on day release. Today he is one of our successful shop managers.

He started us thinking, and knowing that a significant proportion of offenders had been children in the care system, we established our Timpson Foundation to help more people like Matthew. We didn't just give ex-offenders a job, we provided the funds to set up home and get re-established in society. Our disciple was Dennis, a kind, burly man who works in our People Support department, and is also a football referee and a prison visitor. Dennis created links with over 25 prisons, and within three years he had interviewed 100 prisoners and employed 24. We asked Dennis to be tough as well as kind, as we only wanted superstars. From a prison population of over 80,000 we could pick the cream of the crop. For three years we kept things quiet, worried about what colleagues would think, but a headline in *The*

Sun revealed our secret: 'CONS TAUGHT TO CUT KEYS'. I responded on the front page of our *Timpson Weekly News*: THE SUN WON'T STOP US.

We've been surprised at the support our colleagues have given. 'Bill is fantastic,' said one manager of an ox-offender. 'Sue is my best apprentice,' said another. 'Can you find more where they came from?' asked an Area Manager. To encourage other businesses to follow suit, James organised a conference at the Justice Ministry. In his opening remarks, Prison Minister, David Hanson, argued that employment is the key to reducing re-offending and Prison Chaplain, Robin Jenkins, commented that prisoners re-offend because they get no support and no job.

George, who became a Timpson employee, moved the audience into emotional silence.

'I am not proud of what I did. I was an antique dealer having a difficult time and I was offered £20,000 to bring a cocaine-filled suitcase from Grenada. I was arrested at Gatwick, got five years and lost my wife and family. Prison was hard. The violence and intimidation was unbelievable and I had nothing to live for. I stuck to the rules and was offered day release. I saw a notice about Timpson and applied for an interview. What would they think of a 50-year-old drug dealer? The following Monday I started an apprenticeship in Tonbridge.

The first task was to go to the bank with the weekend's takings; what trust, £2,500. Timpson gave me a job, paid the deposit on my flat and furnished it. They simply put my life back on track.'

Ex-offenders like George turned our scheme into a success, but we have learned some hard lessons. One person, highly recommended by his governor, was due to join us the week after release but never arrived. Within three days he re-offended. It works much better if prisoners start work on day release before leaving prison. One girl did well until her boyfriend forced her to sell drugs; she had renewed the relationship that had caused the original offence (we learned that relocation can be vital). Another recruit was late and threw 'sickies'. He had the wrong personality and should never have passed his interview.

Any qualms over the scheme were quashed when James planned a celebration party in Las Vegas for our most successful managers. Three were refused entry to the USA – that's how we discovered they had a criminal record. It made us think. If every employee had a perfect past we would have missed out on some of our most successful managers.

In January 2009 we opened a training workshop inside Liverpool Prison with Timpson colleagues, Wayne and Steve, teaching skills from shoe repairs to watch repairs (not key cutting!). We interview the prisoners before they start and again when they are qualified. It was so successful that a second workshop was opened in December 2009 at Wandsworth. James's prison visit in 2004 created a fantastic means to recruit future stars in a meaningful way, many of whom have already become Timpson branch managers.

* * * * *

Our form of social responsibility is to get involved, but we couldn't have helped adoptive parents, the local school or ex-offenders without a business that makes good money. The business must come first and our priority is to look after our good employees who make it work.

Owning a successful company brings the responsibility to use profits wisely. First, look after your family then care for your employees, but always deal with customers and suppliers in the way that you yourself would like to be treated. Success also provides the possibility of helping others, not just to tick the corporate social responsibility box but to pursue causes close to your heart. I think we have proved that you can be nice and make money at the same time.

Chapter Nine

IDEAS THAT WORK

Business success and failure are often judged by the big deals and major landmarks, but behind the scenes there are many little ideas that make a major contribution.

Over the last 35 years I have tried lots of new things. Many haven't worked but a few have made a spectacular contribution to our success. Some have been home grown, but many have come from elsewhere. To draw this book to a close, what follows is a Top 20 list that has survived the test of time and played an important part in our business development.

1. A perfect day

I worry every time I visit a shop with Alex, as some shoe repairers are naturally scruffy and Alex has incredibly high standards of housekeeping. 'Absolutely filthy,' she frequently comments. This is a male thing. Without being sexist I can reveal that our tidiest shops tend to be run by women. We once expected shoe repair shops to be dirty and dishevelled, until 1979 when we had our first housekeeping campaign. As part of a big spring clean I insisted that every branch colleague wore a tie, which is now a symbol that shows you are a member of the Timpson Club. The tie and the uniform that goes with it have helped our colleagues to clean up their act, but with over 850 shops, housekeeping remains a problem. We try to refit each branch every seven years, but a full makeover is an expensive way to bring housekeeping up to date. Every year we had a massive spring clean, but it was pretty ineffective. A lot of colleagues took no notice and some had little idea what spring cleaning meant. Five years ago we stole an idea from Asda – the Perfect Day. Like most good ideas, it was simple. We designate one day in the year as our Perfect Day. We list standards to be achieved and give branch colleagues six weeks to bring everything up to date ready for the big day. During the next two weeks members of the area team judge every branch with the opportunity to win cash prizes, a plaque and plenty of local PR.

During the four weeks before the Perfect Day our Help Desk is driven mad with requests for new display material. The idea works so well that the Perfect Day is now an annual event in the Timpson calendar. We also introduced the idea to our office with similar success. The Timpson office team took their first Perfect Day so seriously that a large sized skip had to be emptied three times in a fortnight. 'If it works so well,' said someone recently, 'why don't you have a Perfect Day every day?' I don't think they quite got the idea!

2. Awards

I love praising superstars. One of the most successful ways to recognise success is an awards ceremony, but we don't hold them every year. Annual events become too routine; we want to make them special. Our awards coincide with big landmarks like our Centenary in 1997 and the Millennium in 2000. Our *ChildLine* and Customer Care Awards in 2004 were held to celebrate raising £1 million for *ChildLine*. Our next event in 2010 coincides with the 50th anniversary of the day I started work at Timpson.

The venue is important; although the Manchester City stadium was successful, a marquee in our garden works best. It gives a wow factor that people like to talk about to their friends. These are formal events run like an Oscar ceremony with three finalists nominated for each award. Everyone brings a partner or a friend and although there is only one winner per category, every runner-up gets a trophy. I realise how important these occasions are when I see trophies proudly displayed in shop windows and pictures of their presentation on the wall. We are creating long-lasting memories that often feature in the local paper and help to improve the business.

3. Suppliers' lunch

I was a buyer in the days of the liquid lunch (one and half hours in the Hare and Hounds at Timperley) and at Christmas received several bottles of wine. It was an accepted part of the buyer/supplier relationship. The Timpson experience was modest compared with the entertainment accepted by British Shoe Corporation buyers who were given gifts much more substantial than the occasional bottle of wine. For most, this activity was well meaning, but when a few bent buyers accepted bribery from sharp salesmen, the practice became unhealthy.

In the 1970s when there were still a significant number of UK shoemakers, home manufacturers were very irritated with the multiple shoe shops buyers who were bringing in an increasing number of imports. That was why I held my first Open Day for suppliers. I invited them to look at all our imports and compare prices to see whether they could do any better. I called it our Link Scheme and gave them a club card which entitled them to visit every shop. My Link Scheme didn't reduce imports but it was good public relations and suppliers found it helpful. I remembered it several years later when I held my first Suppliers' Lunch.

Having accepted so much hospitality many years before, I decided to turn the tables and invited all our main suppliers for lunch. After the meal I gave a talk on our figures and future plans, and finished with some awards to our suppliers of the year. Our Suppliers' Lunch has been so popular that we hold it almost every year. Sometimes I ask them to bring a colleague who is closely involved with the Timpson account, usually a factory operative, someone from the warehouse or a key back office administrator. We rely on our suppliers' support and many of them rely on us as their main source of income. It is important to keep contact and let them know what's happening in our business.

4. Annual report

We are a private business. Alex and I are the only shareholders. Our accounts are not easy to find – the holding company is called Offerhappy, not Timpson. I am happy to keep our figures away from financial journalists and I'm keen to avoid the rich list, but there are plenty of people outside the family who need to know how we are doing, particularly our suppliers (for many, we are their major customer), our colleagues and their families. Although I write an annual report, I don't use outside PR people because I want to reveal the facts in a way that reflects our culture. Unlike a public company I can produce easy-to-read figures without the interference of stock exchange guidelines. The report is written to satisfy my colleagues, not the City. Writing it makes me think; it provides another excuse to update our strategy. The report is sent to every colleague's home with a personal note and produced as near to the year end as possible. I use plain language and plenty of pictures, as I want all our stakeholders to get a regular health check on company progress.

5. Good news notes

At the end of 1995, following the purchase of Automagic, the company had increased in size from 215 to 325 shops. I realised that being bigger had its problems: there was a danger that I would become too remote from the day-to-day business. I sent everyone a notepad to be used to send comments directly to the Chairman, but they were almost too successful.

Every Monday morning I had a pile of problems sent from all over the country, and it proved to be quite a depressing way to start the week. I then had another idea: I sent another notepad headed 'Good News'. 'Dear John,' it started, 'here is good news ...', with a gap for colleagues to send me something cheerful. The first week I got six back, record turnovers, the biggest ever sale to one customer and one from a colleague whose wife had just had a baby. Ten further pieces of good news arrived the following week. I put everything I had heard so far in a circular to all shops and gave £25 for the best news of the week. That brought a good response, so I started sending a weekly list of good news, always awarding a £25 prize. A few weeks later I tried another idea, an 'Amaze Me' week. I offered to split £1,000 between the colleagues who amazed me most. Replies flooded in on the 'amaze me' notepad. I had found a great way to gather our company news. I turned my good news circular into a newsletter that has grown to 16 pages every week. *Timpson Weekly News* has now passed its tenth anniversary and still uses good news notes to find out what is happening around the business.

6. Summits

Although I don't like meetings I thoroughly enjoy what we call summits – informal discussions with a group of branch colleagues who really know about our customers. We always have a list of problems: How can we cut more of the technical car keys? How do we expand the watch repair business? Can we find a new twist to Customer Care training? These are problems searching for ideas, and although Upside Down Management allows individuals the freedom to use their initiative to try ideas, it isn't very easy to discover what is going on as people tend to keep their ideas to themselves.

Summits have often revealed a solution. The experts who join our discussion group are pulled out of the business – not picked on seniority, but based on knowhow. The trick is to get them talking. Allow at least two hours; it usually takes 45 minutes before they have the confidence to open up their minds. All I have to do is listen, and learn more about my business. A series of summits played a vital role in the development of our watch repair business, not only did the people come up with the ideas but they were also the first people to put those ideas into practice. I love doing new things, but I can't innovate on my own. Experts from around the business have helped us turn ideas into reality.

7. Activity conferences

We hold regular area managers' conferences, but for years we ran them badly. We were keen to tell these key members of our team everything. We paraded a procession of middle managers who were keen to talk about their job, but the area managers were not so keen to listen. The bit of the conference they really enjoyed was the time spent at the bar. We eventually realised that the social part of the conference brought most benefit.

An area manager's life can be lonely. They enjoyed meeting colleagues from other parts of the country who did the same job, but they didn't look forward to the area managers' conference because it was so boring. We decided to make it a lot more fun. Today we provide lots of activity and very little talking, James and I talk about our latest strategy, but most of the time is spent outside the conference room – abseiling, orienteering, motor sports, white-water rafting, a visit to a tannery in Germany, archery, clay pigeon shooting, and many more. When they get home several area managers now send us an e-mail saying, 'Thanks for a great conference.' They learn a lot more from a 10-mile walk with their peers than they ever discovered during a day of PowerPoint presentations.

8. Chairman's award

The standard typewritten 'well done' letter, or a predetermined award set by company guidelines, is worth little, you can't praise people properly by following a set of rules. To mean something, praise must be individual and it is most powerful when it comes out of the blue. E-mails have put a premium on the handwritten letter, that's why I invented my Chairman's Award, a compliment with no rules attached. I simply send a cheque, generally between £50 and £100 (tax paid), with a handwritten letter explaining the reasons why I want to say 'well done'. There is no structure to the Chairman's Award. It's not fair – but I don't care. I send cheques at random if I hear that someone has done something special. The money involved hasn't been budgeted but I don't mind overspending if the cash is going to a star performer.

The Chairman's Award has become a feature of every leadership course. At the end of the first day I ask all delegates if they would like to nominate a colleague for a £100 award. I tell them I have £500 to give away. At the end of the course, those who have put forward a colleague explain why their nominee deserves the award. I usually go well beyond my £500 limit – sometimes I've made over 20 awards, all with a handwritten note. The writer's cramp is well worth it when I receive a 'thank you' or see one of my letters framed the next time I visit the recipient's shop.

9. The people test

Success depends on people. Managers can't do their job unless they know their team very well indeed. From time to time we carry out a People Test, where we ask managers 20 key questions about a colleague. We want to know the name of the colleague's partners, what pets he has, his favourite tipple, which football team he supports, details of his children and his favourite hobbies. Before managers take the test we already have the facts from the colleague concerned. We expect our managers to do well, the test shows how much they know about the people they manage. The game underlines the importance of knowing the personality behind the people you employ. Managers who take a real interest know about their team-mates' well beyond the world of work.

10. Hardship fund

Twenty years ago pilferage used to be an accepted part of the shoe repair package. We tended to turn a blind eye 'as long as we got our share'. Today things are very different. We operate a policy of zero tolerance; whenever fraud is suspected we install a hidden camera and have a six strong security team to check the tapes and catch the criminals. Despite the benevolent way we care for our colleagues we still fire an average of one a week for gross misconduct.

People get into money problems for all sorts of reasons: drugs, credit cards, gambling and divorce, can all cause colleagues to dip into our till. Once they have taken money and got away with it, pilfering can become a habit. We are delighted when we find a dishonest drongo as it means that we can say goodbye immediately, but it is disappointing when one of the best sales people is found guilty, that's why we have a hardship fund. We want people in difficulty to talk to us before things get out of hand. We usually have over £250,000 out on loan to colleagues with money worries (we don't lend a pound to a drongo). It is our policy to trust people and the policy pays off. Over 97% of these loans are repaid in full. We take away temptation and gain a lot of loyalty, as I discovered recently in the Midlands. A branch colleague whose marriage had broken down was amazed at the support we made available. I asked him if he thought I was mad. 'No,' he said, 'you're just eccentric, but it's great to be part of your business because you run it by common sense.'

11. Daily cash check

Profits are important but cash determines whether we or our bankers run the company. We use a simple system to control the cash. Every weekday the bank balance and our total borrowings are e-mailed to my BlackBerry, always compared with exactly the same day last year. This shows, at a glance, the cash we have created or spent in the last 12 months. If I can't explain the difference, I dig more deeply. It is the perfect early warning system; the daily cash check is my most important piece of information and the only report I always look at.

12. Birthdays off

When we celebrated our centenary in 2003 I decided that, as this was a special birthday for the company, every colleague should have a day off for their birthday. If their birthday was on a Sunday or any other non-working day, they could choose another day instead. The idea was so popular that we kept it going and it is now part of the Timpson package. It defines our culture not only to colleagues but to the whole of their family. When I introduced the scheme, an accountant asked me how much it would cost, which I thought was a silly question. This simple benefit has created a lot of goodwill and our colleagues seem to have fewer days off sick; even better, you get to know everyone's birthday so you can send a card, give a present and ring up on the day to wish your team member a happy birthday. Whenever we have bought a new business, most of our perks wait until the acquisition has settled in to the Timpson culture, but we give our new colleagues their birthday off from day one.

13. Interview form

I came up with the idea of our interview form on a train to Euston with my son Edward. We had a problem: while our area managers were recruiting key cutters and shoe repairers, we wanted them to pick personalities, but we couldn't get our message across. The answer was an interview form based around Mr Men. Cartoons of good people, like Mr Happy, Mr Quick, Mr Punctual, Mr Honest and Mr

Keen, were pictured alongside the drongos: Mr Dull, Mr Dishonest, Mr Slow, Mr Late and Mr Sickie. Under each Mr Man was a box to tick, and we asked our area managers to tick those boxes that most resembled the interviewee. They got the message. We are not interested in CVs; nor are we particularly bothered about what candidates say at an interview; we simply assess their character by using my box ticking Mr Men system. It has worked. Our recruiters now know who we are looking for and the business is full of personality.

14. Dreams come true

This is one idea that I didn't copy from someone else – I thought it up myself. To celebrate 20 years since becoming an independent shoe repair company, during which we had grown from 150 to 600 shops, I wrote a booklet and sent a copy to every colleague's home, together with a letter in which I explained that our success was like a dream come true. To celebrate, I promised that every month for the rest of that year we would turn one colleague's dream into reality. The 'dream' suggestions came flooding in and the scheme was so successful that I've kept it going ever since.

So far we have spent about £250,000 on a wide range of dream projects: Trips to Australia to find lost relatives; much needed eye operations; several trips to Disneyland; the purchase of a dog (a particularly expensive breed) desperately wanted by the daughter of one of our key colleagues; a second-hand car; and a mobility vehicle. I was asked by a journalist whether 'Dreams Come True' was driven by business sense or philanthropy. Hard-nosed accountants might see it as an unnecessary cost, but I consider it good business. We are looking after our best employees while adding to the character of the business. Our culture has been created by quirky ideas, and I hope to find many more.

15. Introduce a friend

The best recruiters are our own colleagues. Our 'Introduce a Friend' scheme gives £150 to anyone who introduces a recruit who remains with us for at least 16 weeks and another £250 once they have completed a year. No less than 45% of new Timpson employees come to us through this scheme, which is why we have so many friends and relatives on the payroll. Existing colleagues do the lion's share of our recruitment and bring great people because they introduce friends with a similar personality. They are unlikely to land us with a drongo because they know our business and understand the characters we need. 'Introduce a Friend' brings most of our best apprentices, who tend to stay with the business much longer than other new starters. Perhaps it is time to increase the reward we give to our great group of employment agents.

16. Training in pictures

Our training manuals work because we use pictures rather than words. We started to produce manuals this way because

I myself have great difficulty reading instructions unless they are accompanied by crystal clear illustrations. When writing a manual I draw the picture first and add the words later, cutting the text to as few words as possible. I know it works because I see colleagues reading our manuals in the shops and taking them away at night to do some homework. When my attention moved to management training I used the same technique. Our Mr Men books – How to be a Great Boss, How to Pick Great People, How to Create a Great Team, How to Avoid an Employment Tribunal – and many more, use the same principle. When talking at training courses I use the dreaded PowerPoint, but it is PowerPoint with a difference – all pictures and no words. I just put a picture on the screen and talk about it. We live in a world full of wasted words – manuals that never get read and instructions that are never understood – pictures make all the difference.

17. *Timpson Weekly News*

Our newsletter is an expensive time-consuming project, but it works. If you are looking for the perfect Magic Dust, look no further. Our colleagues take it for granted, but other companies can't believe that we produce two 16-page newsletters every week full of stories about the people in our two businesses, Max Speilmann and Timpson. For 850 shops spread throughout the British Isles, it is a wonderful way to communicate, but the weekly newsletter does much more, it gets rid of our memos and the front page provides me with a regular soap box. We know it's a real success when we see copies of the newsletters lying on the floor of the loo in the back of the shop – that shows they read it. They also take it home so that their families can share the buzz in our business. It is a consistent weekly sign that we are different.

18. Company charity

When I decided to raise money for the NSPCC it did several good deeds at the same time. Customers liked putting a pound in the box for the small jobs, such as putting a hole in a belt, and our colleagues were so keen to support the NSPCC that they started arranging fundraising events of their own. It helped me too, because I had the perfect answer to the constant stream of charitable requests sent to my office.

Despite all the good we are doing, I am sometimes asked whether it is good for business. You can't judge everything by your management accounts, and that's why we have two levels of profit. Our trading profit shows what we earn from our day-to-day activities, but our net profit (the figure you will see in our accounts) is struck after spending some of our trade surplus on extra pensions, special bonuses and charitable projects. A company culture is created by the way it openly demonstrates its values, and having a company charity is a fundamental part of the culture at Timpson.

19. The leadership course

Despite our success I have one main worry: How long will our success last? So many well-known names have disappeared from the High Street and even the most successful companies go through difficult times if management loses the plot. I fear that future generations will forget how we created our success and return to traditional methods, led by a professional manager. If our company fell into the hands of a leader who didn't 'get it', all our achievements over the past 20 years could be undone in a matter of months.

One of my answers was to write a book called *How to Ride a Giraffe*, which sets out in detail the secrets behind our success, but not everyone reads books and I wanted to make absolutely sure that all members of our management team understood the way we at Timpson run our business. That is why James and I launched ourselves on a training series we called, 'The Leadership Course'. This was a 24-hour lunch-time to lunch-time session during which we outlined the detail of Upside Down Management. We started with the directors and area managers and are now talking to branch managers. It is fairly informal, and we try to ensure that everyone enjoys the experience. It helps us to keep our culture up to date and, by talking to everyone face to face, I hope the culture becomes so well established that the business will be run in the same way 20 years from now.

20. Write a book

If you really want to get to know more about yourself and your business – write a book. It takes a long time, but it makes you do a lot of thinking. You get to know more about what works and what doesn't work, and you begin to analyse past failures and successes. You start writing the book to help others to understand your business, but you, personally, will learn a lot while you write it.

*   *   *   *   *

All these ideas have helped to improve our business and some of them could help your company. Don't look for the reasons why they won't work – just give them a go.

CONCLUSION

To be successful in business you need a little luck and I have had more than my fair share. Thanks to my great grandfather I have never had to go for a job interview and, following an odd quirk of fortune, I have, for the last 19 years, owned 100% of my business – an excellent way to ensure job security. I have been helped along the way by Alex's advice, James' talent and his sense of tradition (last year he tracked down and bought the Bristol car that my father was forced to leave at the office when he was ousted as Chairman).

With a career full of so much good fortune I have little to complain about, but I am conscious that this book contains lots of criticism. I make no apology for continually complaining about red tape and regulations. If we don't fight back, the growth of our bureaucratic culture will make life impossible for the true entrepreneur. We have become a compliant nation, buckling under EU directives and pandering to the politically correct agenda. It's amazing that the spirit of free enterprise is still alive and kicking.

Risk-averse management leads to loads of internal rules and regulations – companies are run from Head Office and the country is controlled by Westminster. The administrators sit behind a desk writing policy in the belief that a perfect solution can be produced by insisting that everyone follows the proper process. It gets worse: an increasing number of regulations are issued on behalf of the green agenda, social responsibility and ethical trading. Some objectives soon become less important than the process itself – putting out the correct wheelie bin on the right day is becoming a major measure of citizenship.

Corporate Social Responsibility could become a cynical public relations tool, while 'ethical trading' is a term used with moral hypocrisy. I don't think you can force people to be generous or have a legal requirement to be a do-gooder. I am not going to be bullied into a politically correct agenda in which I do not believe.

Being a family business brings a big advantage. I can do it my way. No one is going to tell me how to be generous, apart from Alex! But having a profitable business provides us with an amazing privilege: it has given us the chance to care for our colleagues, raise a substantial sum for *ChildLine*, support *Ex Offenders* and work with *After Adoption*.

Our upside down style flies in the face of modern 'professional' management. Most gurus praise the importance of delegation but few practise what they preach. They don't trust employees enough to give them real authority. We do!

By picking people with personality, and trusting them to get on with their jobs in the way they know best, the whole atmosphere in our business changed. We suddenly became a team with a common purpose. We have all (company and colleagues) made more money and had a lot more fun along the way. By giving colleagues freedom and trust, James and I have been released from controlling the detail and have the space to be entrepreneurs. We spend much of our time visiting the business, meeting colleagues, watching what they do and listening to their ideas, problems and criticisms. Our diaries are free to do the real job, thinking through the strategy, communicating our culture and doing the deals needed to develop the business.

We look after our superstars with holiday homes, giving them a day off on their birthday and making some of their dreams come true. When they have personal problems we are happy to help, and if they are in financial difficulty we may lend them money. But we don't help everyone – we discriminate against drongos. While most of the business world is writing warning letters and putting their poorest people on performance improvement programmes we simply, and as pleasantly as possible, ask the drongos to go as quickly as possible.

We have used Upside Down Management for over 10 years and have plenty of proof that it works. It is simply the easiest and best way to run our company. While I was writing these final words I visited our shop in Lytham St Annes, where I met the manager, Simon Dodd, who recently rejoined Timpson after a gap of 11 years. 'Has it changed?' I asked.

'What a difference,' he replied. 'It's the support you get from the Area Team and Timpson House and everyone is so friendly. I love the freedom. I feel this is my own shop – I keep telling my friends about Upside Down Management,' and he said after a pause: 'You know, I actually whistle when I drive to work.'

*   *   *   *   *

I have written this book in the hope that others can learn from our experience, and adapt our way of working to their own business. But I suspect few will have the courage to try it.

'It's all right for you,' many will say. 'It may work for a private chain of cobblers but we are not like that.' I disagree. There are bits of our culture that anyone can usefully copy, as long as the CEO 'gets it' and is bold enough to be a bit of a maverick.

Conclusion

I hope, having heard about Upside Down Management, that some readers may be tempted to try it and discover that it is possible to make good money and be nice at the same time.

INDEX

Index compiled by Annette Musker

FINAL THOUGHT

If you are wondering whether we really do run the business according to this book, go along to one of our branches and ask Timpson colleagues what it is like working for an 'upside down' business.

To encourage you to do this bit of research, here is a £5 gift voucher – cut it out and take it with you.

Printed in Great Britain
by Amazon